Missing
in the
Himalayas

Anatomy of an MIA Mission

Dr. Carl Frey Constein

authorHOUSE™

1663 LIBERTY DRIVE, SUITE 200
BLOOMINGTON, INDIANA 47403
(800) 839-8640
WWW.AUTHORHOUSE.COM

First published by AuthorHouse 04/28/05

ISBN: 1-4208-3694-3 (sc)

Printed in the United States of America
Bloomington, Indiana

This book is printed on acid-free paper.

Dedicated to...

the gallant crew of C-46 #996

and

to all WWII airmen killed or missing

in China-Burma-India

Joint POW/MIA Accounting Command
                                          JPAC

"Until they are home"

Contents

Prologue

THE HIMALAYAN HUMP, Nov. 3, 1944. The crew of Curtiss Commando C-46 #996 flies a precious load of gasoline over the Himalaya Mountains to China and is en route back to India at 20,000 feet. At 0300 hours (3 a.m.) just a half-hour from its ETA (Estimated Time of Arrival) at Sookerating, its home base, 996 calls an ominous "Mayday." Ground radio makes frantic attempts to reach the crew. No response. The plane has vanished.

Nearly 60 years pass. A hunter venturing far from his village of Damnya in that exotic autonomous region of China called Tibet stumbles onto chunks of a huge WWII plane that had crashed into a steep cliff. After an investigative team confirms the plane is indeed the missing C-46, JPAC (Joint POW/MIA Accounting Command) in Hawaii sets in motion a high-risk search mission, tasking Army Captain Geoffrey Kent to lead a 14-member recovery team.

∧∧∧

I was excited to learn of this MIA (Missing in Action) mission, for I too was a C-46 Hump pilot flying that terrible November night. Based at Chabua next door to Sookerating, I didn't know the crew of 996, but we Hump airmen were all buddies in spirit—flying the same routes, over the same dense jungles and menacing mountains, in the same terrifying weather. We are deeply grateful to the men of Team Tibet 2004 for braving severe danger and hardship to search for our missing comrades.

I learned about the mission in a fortuitous way. Inspired by Tom Brokaw's *The Greatest Generation* to tell the story of my 96 round-trip Hump flights, I had written the memoir *Born to Fly the Hump*. For background reading as he prepared for the mission, Capt Kent ordered my memoir and a follow-up book of letters entitled *Tales of the Himalayas*. He sent along a note inviting me to dialogue, to become, in essence, a *virtual* member of the team. I was delighted and responded immediately. Replying, he matched my enthusiasm. "I want you and other veterans to know," he wrote, "we are excited about this mission. Our team will represent you in the Himalayas with the same sense of duty, honor, respect, and courage you demonstrated 60 years ago."

What resulted from the captain's invitation is *Missing in the Himalayas*. The book is a detailed anatomy of all phases of this dangerous and rigorous mission, from the nine-month preparation to the team's deployment and ultimate excavation of the crash site. Thanks to electronic technology, I was able to stay in touch with Capt Kent and the team every step of the way—in Hawaii, in Alaska, in Beijing, in Lhasa, in Bayi Town, in Damnya, and, most marvelously, at the site of the crash of 996 at 14,100 feet there on the "Roof of the World" in Tibet. He filled me in on every phase of the mission. I was especially delighted to receive his daily reports as the team left Lhasa and made its perilous way to the crash site and carried out the excavation. And after the team returned to Hawaii, he sent me nearly 100 stunning photographs from the mision.

It's been a thrill and an honor to be the link between Team Tibet 2004 and three buddies missing since 1944. To connect the dots separating these 60 years, I've inserted chapters briefing the reader on that little-known WWII airlift operation called the Hump, at places adding my personal take from a momentous year in the China-Burma-India theater of operations.

The story begins with the most dreaded word in a pilot's vocabulary—"*Mayday!*"

Carl Frey Constein

Chapter 1

The Hump
"Mayday! Mayday!"

*A*t the 1337th AAF Base Unit in Sookerating, eastern India, the crew of Curtiss Commando 996 prepared for another three-hour cargo flight to China over towering Himalayan peaks. The date was November 3, 1944. The pilots met in Operations an hour before takeoff, scheduled for 1930 hours (7:30 p.m.). It's likely they had never flown together, for policy ruled out fixed crews. After filing a flight plan, they probably had coffee before being jeeped to their plane awaiting them on the flight line. The radio operator was already at his station behind the cockpit. After making their walk-around inspection, the pilots climbed into the huge transport and worked through the preflight checklist. The copilot called the tower.

"Oboe How, 996 requests taxi instructions."

"Roger, Niner-niner-six, you are cleared to the end of the runway." Alert to the severe penalty for hitting a wingtip of the planes lining the taxiway, the pilot taxied slowly to the takeoff circle. There he and the copilot completed the final checklist, checked the engine magnetos, and called the tower.

"Niner-niner-six," the tower responded, "you are cleared for takeoff. Altimeter 29.32."

The pilot squared up on the runway, shoved the throttles hard, and the big bird lumbered down the runway. When she reached 90 mph, she reluctantly lifted off and 15 seconds later was engulfed in pea *soup. Heading north toward the Sadiya radio beacon, the plane climbed at 300 feet per minute. In 10 minutes the ADF (Automatic Direction Finder) needle did a 180 over the beacon, and the pilot began climbing in a racetrack pattern, continuing until the plane reached 10,000 feet. After clearing the First Ridge, the Patkai Range, the crew put on oxygen masks and turned southeast to the "Easy" route, continuing their climb. When they reached 18,500 feet over Shingbwiyang, Burma, the pilot turned on the autopilot; the engines purred contentedly. The plane crossed a series of 14,000-16,000-foot ridges. Passing over the next radio checkpoint at Paoshan in China's high Santsung Range, they turned due east toward Kunming. In 90 minutes 996 would deliver its precious load of twenty-two 55-gallon drums of gasoline for General Chennault's 14th Air Force or for the Chinese Army.*

The pilots chatted about this and that as they flew on. In their early 20s, 12,000 miles from home, they talked mostly about the girls back home. Behind the bulkhead, the radio operator had little time to dream as he kept in touch on his liaison set with the 4th wing of the Army Airways Communication System. Above a solid lid of stratus clouds, the crew enjoyed the smooth ride.

Three hours after takeoff, pushed along by the benign 75-mph Prevailing Westerly wind, 996 was over Kunming. The pilot turned to 58 degrees to approach Chanyi. "Charlie Yoke, 996 requests landing instructions. Over."

"Roger Niner-niner-six, descend to 12,000 feet and hold," the Chanyi tower ordered.

The ride suddenly became bumpy as the plane entered a thick overcast. Flying on instruments, 996 was on top of a stack of planes from ATC's (Air Transport Command) bases in India. Each aircraft was instructed to hold its altitude until directed to descend 500 feet after the lowest plane in the stack had landed. When their turn came to land, the crew of 996 saw land for the first time on the flight, just 15 seconds before landing. The touchdown was smooth.

A mile high, Chanyi has a pleasant climate with a balmy breeze year-round. The pilots strolled to the chow line for a bite to eat. "Ek-ess, Cho?" the Chinese cook asked every GI Joe in line, even though eggs were all there was on the menu. After they'd eaten, the pilots returned to Old Dumbo to relieve the radio operator of guard duty so he too could enjoy the famous "flied ek-ess" and delicious bread.

    In an hour the plane was unloaded, and at 1137 hours 996 took off on its return flight, this trip empty, on a more northerly course, climbing to an altitude of 20,000 feet. Bucking the normal 75-mph west headwind, the crew planned a four-hour flight, ETA at Sookerating—0330 hours. "All aboard for Sook," the pilot may have joshed. "Ding Hao!"

CFC: In a remarkable connection, I had my first flight, my initiation to the Hump, on that same night, November 3, 1944. I clearly recall the weather at takeoff from Chabua—hard rain, wind, lightning and thunder. "We aren't going to take off in this stuff?" I'd asked the pilot as we had coffee in Operations after filing a flight plan. "Hell, this isn't bad," he replied. He needed just one last flight to reach 600 hours and head stateside. His last flight, my first.

    Suddenly as we climbed over the First Ridge toward cruising altitude, the left engine backfired, knocking so hard I feared it would break off. Just as the pilot was about to call a Mayday and feather the props, the engine settled down. "Well, I'm not nursing this bastard all the way to China, tonight," he said as he turned Old Dumbo around and barreled back into the vicious storm. After a scary 20-minute ride in the storm, we came in for a routine landing. My first Hump trip lasted one hour—a flight to nowhere.

    Had we gone on to China and back that night, I could report precisely on the weather 996 faced on its flight home. Lacking that, I make the assumption the plane flew into extraordinarily violent storms like some I experienced on my 96 round-trips. To speculate further, had our left engine not hiccupped, had we not aborted our flight to China, the disaster that awaited 996 might also have been ours.

    The air was a bit choppy as 996 flew over Yunnanyi, 132 miles west of Chanyi, on its westerly route, named "Charlie." Then, without warning, the plane barged into a gigantic cumulonimbus storm rising to 40,000 feet, spitting out blazing streaks of lightning. St. Elmo's Fire, harmless but scary, danced on the props and the instrument panel. Golf balls of hail bounced off the fuselage, loud thumps punctuating the rolling thunder. Thick ice covered the windshield and the wings. The C-46 became a child's toy, driving through violent squalls of torrential rain and blinding snow. Prop deicers slung huge volleys of ice against the windows. Airspeed jumped from near stalling at 80 mph to a red-lined 260 mph as sharp gusts and wind shear pushed the plane up, then down, then sideways. The ADF needle spun like a top as the crew desperately sought the next radio checkpoint, Shingbwiyang, Burma, the pilot holding to a course of 287 degrees.

Three hours into the flight, 996 called out "Mayday! Mayday!" Ground radio attempted repeatedly to reach the crew. But 996 did not acknowledge. The plane had vanished.

∧∧∧

What went wrong? Likely scenarios, some interrelated:
- *An engine failed.*
- *ADF radio signals were not functioning properly.*
- *Preempting the faithful Prevailing Westerlies, a wind of 100 mph or greater blew out of the south or southwest, pushing 996 far to the north.*
- *Heavy ice formed on the wings and destroyed the airfoil. Loss of lift resulted in loss of altitude.*
- *Carburetor ice caused the engines to lose power.*
- *The plane ran out of fuel.*

The plane crashed in Tibet, just six miles north of the border with India. On its fateful flight that November night, off course, running out of fuel, the engines sputtering, 996 was doomed. I feel the terror of that gallant crew.

All of us who flew the Hump had our own Maydays. I recall one terrible flight when we put the plane on auto pilot and prepared to hit the silk when, suddenly, miraculously, we flew out of the horrendous storm, the left engine stopped its spitting and coughing, and we rushed back to the cockpit. Those of us who survived the Hump were not better pilots than the men of 996—we were luckier!

Chapter 2

Amazing Discoveries in Tibet

Fastforward 55 years. Near the remote Tibetan village of Damnya, a local hunter comes upon a WWII Army Air Corps plane, its parts crushed and scattered on a snow-covered mountainside. The word goes out to Chinese authorities. The following year, two Tibetans from the village of Langko spot a second crash, remarkably just 30 miles from the Damnya site. Both planes were Curtiss C-46s used on the Himalayan Hump airlift. For six decades the planes and their crews presumably lay scattered on mountain cliffs, covered in winter by snowy blankets.

Photo by Dr. Tyrell

September 3, 2004. Wreckage of C-46 #996 in the southeast corner of Tibet. The other Tibetan crash site, excavated in 2002, lies 30 miles west. Both sites will soon be covered by heavy snows blanketing the high peaks of the Himalayas.

The People's Republic of China (PRC) directs the Foreign Office of the Tibet Autonomous Region (TAR) to send a reconnaissance team to the sites. (In 1951 China had forced out the Dalai Lama and regained control of Tibet.) The planes are located in the rugged, extremely sparsely populated terrain of Southeast Tibet—one at 15,700 feet, the other at 14,100 feet. In a welcome and astute stroke of international cooperation at the start of the new millennium, the Chinese government informs Washington of the discoveries. The U.S. Central Identification Laboratory in Honolulu orders a 14-member team to excavate the crash sites and assigns Army Captain Daniel Rouse Team Leader.

In July 2002 the team deploys to Lhasa, fabled capital of the TAR. After a week adjusting to high altitude, the team embarks on a six-day trek to the village of Langko. From there, after four days of strenuous walking and horseback riding through 32 miles of extremely rugged mountain terrain, the team sets up camp at 14,000 feet; the plane, missing since March 1944, lies 1,700 feet higher. Excavating the Langko site, the team recovers more than 100 pieces of bone and dental remains.

Plans of the Rouse team to excavate the second site 30 miles to the east are cancelled when heavy winter weather sets in. But before the team leaves the mountain, an investigative squad is deployed to locate and survey the Damnya site for a future JPAC excavation. In the squad is mountaineer Mark Gilbertson, who will later be a member of the 2004 MIA team. After a couple days' walk, the four-man party reaches a village, from which they travel by vehicle to Milin. The next day they drive to Damnya, remaining overnight. From there they begin a strenuous four-day hike higher and higher into the mountains, ultimately reaching the crash site.

C-46 #996 had crashed into a cliff at 14,100 feet. Incredibly harsh, mountainous, and isolated, the site is much less accessible than the 15,700-foot Langko site the Rouse team had excavated. The tree line is at 13,000 feet. The party crosses two icy and swollen rivers, one just outside Damnya several times.

"It was like winning the jackpot, getting up there and finding these two planes," said Capt Rouse after the team returned to headquarters in Hawaii. Dr. James T. Potkines, the team's anthropologist, added, "This is very, very rugged, sparsely populated terrain. There aren't a lot of people to find them."

CFC: Anthropologist Potkines is quoted in press releases as saying he believed the four crewmen died instantly, but if they had survived the impact, instant depressurization would have killed them. Actually, C-46s were not pressurized. Above 10,000 feet, crews used oxygen masks.

∧∧∧

After receiving his orders for the Damnya excavation, Capt Kent wasted no time laying out priorities. The mission was planned for the summer of 2003, but when a SARS epidemic hit China the mission was postponed to 2004.

Capt Kent learned that an effort to locate the missing C-46 had been made shortly after the crash in 1944. An Army Air Corps (AAC) search and rescue pilot sighted what he believed to be the plane resting on the side of an "almost vertical cliff" in China at 8,000 feet near the Mekong River. The American Graves Registration Service notified families of the crew that the C-46 had been found and that inaccessibility of the site precluded recovery. Declared administratively dead as of the date of missing and their remains declared non-recoverable, they were memorialized on the Tablet of the Missing at Manila American Cemetery. Considering the case closed, AAC conducted no further investigation. A half-century later, the plane was finally found 400 miles west and north of the Mekong.

CFC: I was not surprised to learn of the faulty sighting, for search and rescue on the Hump was not a planned, well-organized or well-staffed operation. What this search and rescue pilot spotted must have been another wreckage. But recording it as a plane known even then to be two hours past the Mekong River on its flight west is inexplicable.

Ironically, a search and rescue unit came into being initially not to treat and rescue downed Hump airmen but as a result of the bailout of several VIP American civilians and high-ranking Chinese Army officers headed from India to China. They jumped into the Burmese jungle from a disabled C-46, all but the copilot successfully. The best-known passenger was CBS correspondent Eric Severeid. Responding to an urgent

17

request for medical help, three medics were dropped. After a 16-day trek through thick jungle, a rescue team finally reached the downed party, which had been supplied by airdrops.

Publicity about the dramatic rescue demonstrated the value of a search and rescue unit. But there appeared to be no sense of urgency. In the fall of 1943 Capt Blackie Porter, an experienced C-87 pilot, volunteered to start a unit. Appointed Air Rescue Officer at Chabua, he enlisted three pilots and a few enlisted men, then found, or perhaps appropriated, two old C-47s, and salvaged two B-25s and an L-5.

In his 1964 book Over the Hump, *Gen William H. Tunner* wrote that when he came to India to take over the Hump operation, Washington approved his plan for a CBI (China-Burma-India) Search and Rescue unit to replace the "cowboy operation a few dedicated, brave, hard-working men had been carrying out. The number of rescue planes was doubled. We now had an efficient, military Search and Rescue Unit dedicated to its task on a steady, thoroughgoing basis."

Esprit de corps is crucial in military organizations. I was amazed to read after the war that there was such an S&R unit on the Hump—even more amazed because it was apparently based at the 1333rd Base Unit at Chabua, where I was stationed for one year! I have to wonder why our Chabua air crews were not told of this. It would have been good for morale to know, in addition, that every base was directed to establish a jungle indoctrination camp for aircrews, and that local tribesmen in North Burma had been organized to find and rescue downed American airmen.

Rescue was only one of the missions of secret OSS Detachment 101 that operated in the CBI theater of war. In his book Green Hell Harry Hengshoon—his code name was "Skittles"—a behind-the-lines civilian agent of the detachment, tells of the group's unconventional operations against Japanese forces .in Burma. Through infiltration, disguise, evasion, and communication, the 900-man detachment rescued 25 Allied airmen and killed 5,400 Japanese troops (known losses) and estimated an additional 10,000 Japanese troops killed or wounded. The detachment demolished 57 bridges, derailed nine trains, and destroyed/captured 15,000 vehicles.

I am grateful to Detachment 101 and to U.S. pilots, crews and medics who helped rescue or who tended to downed airmen. I know of no firm statistics on this. But clearly, search and rescue was not an early priority, never a top priority. Perhaps other Hump bases did more to make their pilots aware of such important information. As a pilot at Chabua, I, for one, felt expendable.

The Search and Rescue pilot who erroneously reported 996 near the famous Mekong River made an honest mistake. To make a thorough search for the crew and excavate the crash site in Tibet required the resources of the Defense Department's Joint POW/MIA Accounting Command based at Hickam AFB, Honolulu. A year earlier, the Central Identification Laboratory in Hawaii had been merged with the Joint Task Force—Full Accounting to form JPAC, a 425-person organization of handpicked soldiers, sailors, airmen, marines, navy, and civilians. Like the Hump and the CBI, JPAC is little known.

The Command's highest priority is the return of living Americans who remain prisoners of war. To account for all Americans missing as a result of the nation's wars—77,000 from WWII alone, including 416 CBI fliers—JPAC analyzes prospective cases, negotiates with foreign governments, investigates and excavates recovery sites, and identifies and returns to families any recovered remains and artifacts.

JPAC selects cases for recovery based on analysis of intelligence, the host country's political stability, weather, site accessibility, logistics, supportability, and safety. JPAC's mantra, *"Until They are Home,"* speaks to the profound desire for closure by families of MIAs and to the nation's deep sense of reverence and honor for its war dead and missing.

CFC: A personal note of remembrance. Capt. Kent and other JPAC personnel are stationed at Hickam Air Force Base. Geoff and his family live a block from Pearl Harbor itself. Daughter Emily goes to an elementary school next to a water tower Japanese pilots spared because they thought it was a church.

I go back to Sunday, December 7, 1941. On my way to see my girlfriend in Reading, PA, I stopped for gas for my old 1931 Chevy coupe and learned from the attendant that Japan had attacked Pearl Harbor, Schofield Barracks, and Hickam Field. I find this full-circle coincidence amazing—that the Army captain and the JPAC team tasked to recover WWII flying buddies of mine are based at Hickam! I knew on that awful December Sunday day I'd be going off to war. I could not have imagined I'd become a pilot, fly the Himalayas, and 60 years later experience the supreme gratification of having an MIA recovery team <u>based at Hickam</u> search in Tibet for missing buddies of mine.

Chapter 3

Getting Started

A day after his appointment as Team Leader, Capt Kent went into full-court press in his office at Hickam AFB—getting organized to assess, to plan, to procure staff and equipment, and generally to manage the mission. He tackled the immediate task of scheduling flights to Beijing, China, and Lhasa, Tibet, for negotiations and later for carrying team members and cargo. As it happened, another JPAC team was excavating a crash site in China near the North Korean border. Capt Kent scheduled delivery of his team's equipment to Beijing to coincide with the conclusion of that excavation so the China team could return to Hawaii in the same military plane.

He devoted early days to research and planning—agenda for negotiations in China, routes to the crash site and camps, site excavation, medical evacuation, logistical support, staff training, communications from the site, redeployment, returning the remains. He selected and procured required equipment.

Capt Kent made hand-picking of team members a top priority. All were volunteers, all selected for their experience, maturity, professionalism, and mental/physical toughness. He was assisted in this task by Sergeant First Class Mike Swam, his non-commissioned officer in charge, (U.S. Army, Mortuary Affairs Specialist, Ranger Qualified). From the JPAC unit there at Hickam, Capt Kent quickly grabbed two who were on the 2002 Tibet team—Gunnery Sergeant

Chris Behn, (USMC, Explosive Ordnance Disposal Specialist) and Master Sergeant Rocky Keohuhu-Bolor (Special Forces Medic) as team medic. Rocky was difficult to procure because in his position as NCOIC of the Medical Section he does not generally deploy. For Anthropologist/Recovery Leader, Geoff chose Dr. Andrew Tyrell, accomplished climber experienced in many MIA missions. Dr Tyrell is a civilian on the JPAC staff.

As on past missions, JPAC had to go outside its organization for "augmentees" to fill needed slots. For team medical doctor, Capt Kent pursued and got a talented flight surgeon, Maj Karl Larsen, head of Orthopedics at the Air Force Academy. An accomplished climber, Dr. Larsen has extensive experience working in remote sites. He arrived in Hawaii a few days before the important briefing of the commanding general so he could respond to questions about medical care and medical evacuation.

Capt Kent's neighbor, an Air Force Combat Rescue Officer, helped him locate top Air Force pararescueman Staff Sergeant Gabriel Sema of the 31st Rescue Squadron, Kadena Air Base, Okinawa. JPAC has Vietnamese and Korean linguists on its staff, but no Chinese linguists. The request that went out to the Marine Corps, Pacific, resulted in two linguists from Okinawa. (One of the two later washed out during the intensive mountain training in Alaska and was returned to his unit. No urgent requirement for a replacement, the team therefore consisted of 13 members when it deployed to Tibet.)

Team Tibet 2004

Team Leader	Capt Geoff Kent (Army)
Recovery Leader	Dr. Andy Tyrell (civilian)
Asst. Team Leader	SFC Mike Swam (Army)
Team Doctor*	Maj Karl Larsen (USAF)
Medic	MSG Rocky Keohuhu-Bolor (Army)
Pararescue Specialist*	SSGT Gabriel Serna (Marine)
Explosives Specialist	GySGT Chris Behn (Marine)
Linguist*	LCPL Ng (Marine)
Mountaineer*	SSG Gary Beemster (Army)
Mountaineer*	Mark Gilbertson (civilian)
Photographer	SGT Ricardo Morales (Marine)
Mortuary Specialist	SSG Mike Harris (Army)
Mortuary Specialist	SGT Alfred Castro (Army)

Capt Kent discovered early that maps of Tibet are hard to come by; he was able to order a few through the National Imaging and Mapping Agency. A retired Department of Defense official with imagery experience put him in contact with a company called *Space Imaging,* which graciously provided six free images of the site. The company typically charges $2500 an image.

Next on Capt Kent's agenda came team physical training in Oahu in April/May for strength and endurance—prerequisites to mountain training in Alaska. The training was intense, focusing on leg strength, endurance, and cardio exercise. <u>Mondays</u> were given to pull exercises for back and biceps; <u>Tuesdays</u> to exhausting 4-hour hikes with an average gain of 2,500 feet; <u>Wednesdays</u> to leg weights and 5-mile runs; <u>Thursdays</u> were "Triahlon" days (swim 25 minutes, bike 10-15 miles, run two miles), followed in the afternoon by push exercises, (chest, shoulders and triceps) for upper body strength; <u>Fridays</u> were hike days with lighter pack, shorter distance and time.

Tuesday hikes were conducted at four mountain locations: Shafter: Schofield/PlDC Trail, Trippler, and Lanipo. In five hikes of 12 hours 28 minutes, the team climbed 9,650 feet with an average rate of ascent of 14.5 meters per minute.

Polanipor Ridge, Hawaii. (L to R) Ssgt. Harris, Sfc. Swam, Capt. Kent and Sgt. Castro take a break from physical training before going to Alaska for mountain training.

Team Tibet 2004. Back row (l to r): Morales, Keohuhu-Bolor, Harris, Larsen, Serna, Swam, Gilbertson, Kent, Tyrell.
Front row: Ng, Behn, Castro, Beemster

Chapter 4

Leaders of the Team

Geoff Kent, leader of Team Tibet 2004, grew up in Falls Church, Virginia. He and Aimee, his childhood sweetheart, celebrated their ninth wedding anniversary in September, Geoff on the mountain in Tibet, Aimee back home in Pearl Harbor with their two girls. (Later, in a call to Geoff at the crash site in Tibet, Aimee informed him they'd be having an addition to the family.) The Kents live a block from the famous harbor; Geoff's office is nearby at Hickam Air Force Base. Daughter Carolyn is 3. Emily, aged 6, attends school next to an old, historically significant water tower.

Geoff graduated from the University of Alabama in 1994 with a major in criminal justice and a minor in English. He considered federal law enforcement as a career, but it just didn't work out. He wanted more structure and discipline in his life, so, having been in ROTC in college, when Desert Storm came along he volunteered for active duty.

His intention was to serve one regular tour, but Geoff ended up sticking around. With 10 years' service under his belt, he anticipates serving 20 years or more. Before coming to the Central Identification Laboratory in Hawaii in the summer of 2002, he was a Company Commander in the 101st Airborne Assault Division at Fort Campbell, Kentucky. After three years, the Department of the Army moves officers into new assignments for career progression. The assignment manager told him, "Geoff, if you'd be interested in MIA recovery work and your family would like to live in Hawaii, I've got a great job for you." Aimee agreed and they were off to live on the paradise island of Oahu.

Having been Team Leader for MIA missions to Laos and Vietnam, and having been to North Korea and China for mission negotiations, Geoff was moved up to JPAC's China/North Korea Desk. Even before having been bitten by the climbing bug during training on Mt. McKinley in Alaska, he had eagerly looked forward to going to the Himalayas, especially to Tibet, that fabled and forbidden land. (Tibet, no longer independent, is known as the highest—average altitude 12,000 feet—and the sparsest country in the world.) Geoff had always been an outdoorsman and physical fitness buff, but he hadn't done much hiking—until he came to Oahu.

"Oahu is crowded," he said, "but when you disappear into the mountains, just minutes from the base, and not a soul is around, you sit on a ridge, look down and take in the beauty of the island. And you think, 'How can there be no other people up here?'"

Geoff has headed two MIA Vietnam missions, one in Quang Binh Province, the second in Vung Tau near Saigon. In the first, the team found bone but didn't have enough DNA for identification. In the second, the team made two positive IDs, one of a pilot who had been partially recovered after his plane crashed in 1960. The crash site was located in a mangrove swamp that required ditches around the swamp to dry it out. He considers the mission a great recovery, capped by the finding of the pilot's class ring.

Conditions in Vietnam, Cambodia, and Laos could not be more different from what the team will find in Tibet. The jungle technique of digging deep for remains will not be feasible in the high elevation of mountainous Tibet. Geoff expects the Tibet mission to be the most daunting and dangerous JPAC has undertaken.

Geoff had been aware that his name, together with a number of other JPAC-experienced Team Leaders, was being tossed around for this mission, the second act of a Tibet recovery drama. He pursued the assignment zealously. When the mission was scrubbed because of a SARS epidemic in China in 2003, Geoff nevertheless kept on it, planning, keeping it on the scope while everyone else was thinking about other missions. Even while deployed on missions to Vietnam, he maintained the visibility of Tibet, planning for other China and North Korea missions. As JPAC began scheduling for the new fiscal year, Kent pushed the new Tibet mission and pressed to be Team Leader.

Geoff said, "As a soldier, I am comforted in knowing that should I make the ultimate sacrifice while serving my country, there are servicemen and civilians like the professionals I am working with who will continue to search until I am home."

Sergeant First Class Michael Swam, whose Military Occupational Specialty is Mortuary Affairs (MA), is the "team sergeant," the non-com in charge for Team Tibet 2004, Capt Kent's right-hand man. Veteran of 33 MIA missions, he has been, among other assignments, to Africa, Santos (in the Pacific), Guatemala, Panama, Germany, North Korea, Russia, Vietnam, Laos, and Cambodia. Because of Mike's wide experience, Geoff sought him for this extremely hazardous mission to Tibet.

After high school, Mike enrolled in college, played football, did long-line fishing for a while, and then enlisted for active duty in the Army. He'd wanted the Airborne Rangers but was rejected because he's colorblind. Given a variety of Military Occupations to choose, he'd sought his parents' advice. A funeral home in town promised him a job after he got out of the service; he selected MA so he could fall back on that offer if or when he decided to leave the military.

Trained as MA at Fort Lee, Virginia, for two months, Sgt Swam first served from 1988 to 1990 in Fort Ord, California. He went to the desert to serve in Desert Shield, then headed inbound to Hawaii in December, 1991. In June 2001 he was transferred to Fort Lee as instructor. A year ago he was sent back to Hawaii.

He explained that some MAs, mostly stationed at Fort Lee, are assigned at the regular company level, working in the "real world" at collection points or evacuation points to process remains on the battlefield, as in Iraq and Afghanistan today. Most MAs work at JPAC on recovering MIAs. Mike estimates that 80 percent of MIA recovery missions he's been on were successful in retrieving remains. His job is to assist the anthropologist in processing remains. After he defines the site, the anthropologist determines the size of grids—1x4 meters, 5x5 meters, whatever he determines is appropriate for that site. Mike recalled one site in Germany laid out in 10x10 meter grids. On this Tibet mission, he said, there will be the usual sieving for remains but very little digging of dirt.

"When it comes to that phase of the recovery," Mike said, "everyone on the team pitches in, regardless of his specialty or rank." If a large piece of remains is found, the anthropologist is called over immediately. Small pieces are put in a zip-lock plastic bag and dropped in a bucket for the anthropologist to examine at break time.

The Tibet mission will be Mike's first high-altitude mission. "I'm most definitely looking forward to it," he said.

The non-com in charge is 38 years old, has 16 years' military service and plans to go for either a 20- or 35-year retirement. He's married—his wife is from Hawaii—and has sons 19 and 26 and a grandson from his wife's prior marriage. He takes a lot of ribbing about his age on that score. An outdoor person, he enjoys going to the beach, fishing, and taking time with his family.

"Words can't explain," he said, "how rewarding it is for us to do these recoveries. You WWII fellows got this country to where we are right now, that's for sure."

CFC: I interviewed Geoff and other team members by telephone in Hawaii before they deployed to Tibet. To a man I found them engaging conversationalists, energized by their work, particularly by this high-risk mission. Obviously great physical specimens, they are also intelligent professionals committed to honoring America's war-dead and missing. I hope I'll have the chance to meet them all in person.

Connections

I see connections, some personal, some admittedly abstruse, between members of Team Tibet 2004 and me.

-- <u>*Geoff Kent:*</u> *(1)* The name Hickam Field, where Geoff works, was indelibly imbedded in my mind and soul on the afternoon of December 7, 1941. *(2)* Geoff minored in English in college; I spent the best years of my professional life teaching high school students to speak and write. *(3)* Geoff married an Aimee; I married an Amy.

-- <u>*Mike Swam:*</u> We have mutual respect for the courage involved in each other's military careers. He put it this way: "Holy Cow! A Hump pilot at age 21!" My retort: "Endure a month or more at 14,000 feet in the Himalayas without oxygen? No way!"

Chapter 5

<u>The Hump</u>
Why We Were There

*A*ir Transport Command crewmen flew Hump flights
from India to China and back every second or third day.
Round-trip flights averaged seven hours—three hours east to China,
four hours west back to India, the prevailing westerly constantly in
play at 75 mph. So, like long-haul truck drivers, we had plenty of
time to contemplate, to ruminate, to dream. Our thoughts were on
home and those we left behind, never on such weighty matters as
how or why the Hump came into being. In a poem about an earlier
war, Tennyson wrote, "Theirs not to reason why; theirs but to do and
die."

    In the air and at fields we flew into in the CBI, we saw
cargo planes with markings of other commands—Troop Carrier,
Combat Cargo, Air Commandos, CNAC (China National Aviation
Corporation.) And the skies were dotted with even more planes—U.S.
fighters and bombers over Burma and China.

    Of course we understood we were all there to keep China in
the war, but we had to wait until after the war to learn the checkered
story of the Hump/CBI and to read about the CBI's strong-willed,
charismatic personalities—Generalissimo and Madame Chiang
Kai-shek, General Vinegar Joe Stilwell, General Clair Chennault,
General Frank Merrill, British General Orde Wingate, Colonels Phil
Cochran and John Alison.

Strategy for China was laid out at the Arcadia Conference in Quebec shortly after Pearl Harbor by Prime Minister Winston Churchill, President Franklin D. Roosevelt, and Prime Minister Mackenzie King of Canada. In China they found an ally who had been at war with Japan for 10 years in the second Sino-Japanese conflict. The Allies' strategy was three-fold: keep China in the war to prevent the fall of India and Burma, tie up a million Japanese troops that could otherwise be engaged against our troops in the Pacific, and, most urgent of all, hold bases in eastern China as likely jump-off points for the ultimate invasion of Japan.

The China-Burma-India theater of operations was set up in the spring of 1942. For many WWII buffs, it is the most intriguing of all theaters. In their book Thunder Out of China, White and Jacoby write, "The CBI command was the stuff of legends; Americans used to say you needed a crystal ball and a copy of Alice in Wonderland to understand it. CBI politics were a fabulous compound of logistics, personalities, communism, despotism, corruption, imperialism, nonsense, and tragic impotence."

The Allies recognized China as a weak nation with a corrupt central government and autonomous regions controlled by warlords. All-out civil war lay just beneath the surface, but after Japan invaded, warlords who supported Chiang forced a truce between Chiang's Kuomintang and Mao's Communists. Survival of China itself required the moratorium.

China lacked self-sufficient industrial strength. Goods and materiel were imported from Hong Kong, Hanoi, the Soviet Union, and from the west over the famous Burma Road, a 770-mile serpent from Lashio, Burma, to Kunming, China. Built by hand by 100,000 Chinese workers, the road was completed in 1938.

After Pearl Harbor, Japan invaded Rangoon and drove north in Burma. In spite of the sensational "kill" record of the Flying Tigers (American Volunteer Group) in their Curtiss P-40s, Japanese planes severed the Burma Road. The Allies sought alternate ground routes to China from the west, one with a fascinating connection to the 2004 Tibet MIA recovery mission. The American government sought permission from Tibet, an independent nation then, to allow supplies to travel through its territory en route to China. One of the U.S.

envoys, incidentally, was Ilia Tolstoy, grandson of the famous Russian novelist. In their book Lost in Tibet, Starks and Murcutt relate how the U.S. request became inextricably caught up in China vs Tibet politics. Even though the American officials were well received by the Tibetan government, their request for passage was turned down.

When no new ground routes could be negotiated, the only alternative was to fly supplies from India to China over the awesome Himalayas. In Washington, Gen Hap Arnold assured President Roosevelt it could be done, and history's first airlift was born. In the spring of 1942 the entire Air Corps had only 216 transport planes; on the other side of the world and on the bottom rung of priorities, the Hump got what was left over after other commands took their pickings.

The mighty Himalayas on a rare clear day. Hump airmen treasure the memory of their first glimpse.

What became known as "the Hump" got its operational start in a complex, circuitous manner. After the fall of the Dutch East Indies, Maj Gen Louis Brereton, commander of the air units there, came to India with eight heavy bombers and crews. Later, one transport group, a headquarters squadron, and ground support for the tactical groups arrived. Thus began the CBI service of the 10'th Air Force, which had been activated in February at Patterson Field, Ohio.

An air route to China became an early priority of the 10th. To the displeasure of Brereton, the War Department assigned air transport to his chief-of-staff, Brig Gen Earl Naiden. Within the 10th Air Force Naiden set up two ferry commands—the Trans-India to move cargo from Karachi in western India to Assam in eastern India, and the Assam-Burma-China (ABC) to carry supplies over the Himalayas to China. Naiden first proposed flying cargo from the RAF (Royal Air Force) base at Dinjan, Upper Assam Province, to Myitkyina in north Burma. Cargo would then be barged south to Bhamo, Burma, and from there driven over the Burma Road to China.

According to Christy and Shanburger in their book Summon the Stars, *Colonel Caleb Haynes was tasked with organizing the ABC Ferry Command out of Dinjan. Haynes' task force consisted of 13 B-17s, a supporting C-47, and the commander's B-24. The group's original mission had been to bomb Tokyo from a base in China as a follow-up to Col Jimmy Doolittle's planned raid. When the Haynes' mission was scrubbed, the group's bombers were diverted to General Brereton's 10th Air Force. C-47 pilots of Haynes' unit were the first Hump pilots.*

Thus began bitter in-fighting that characterized control of air transportation not only in the CBI but in all theaters. The question was whether air transport should be under the global control of the Air Corps Ferrying Command (later renamed the Air Transport Command) or under control of theater commanders.

The first U.S. cargo-carrying Hump flight by the 10th Air Force was made in support of the audacious, morale-boosting Doolittle raid on Tokyo on April 18, 1942. Sixteen B-25s took off from a carrier in the South Pacific and bombed the Japanese capital. The plan was to land after the raid in eastern China and refuel with gas delivered over the Hump. All 16 planes escaped anti-aircraft hits, but because they were spotted by the enemy and forced to take off before they had arrived at their planned launch site, they ran out of fuel. Most pilots bailed out at night over China.

CFC: Japan meted out merciless revenge on Chinese people in the region where the Raiders landed. James Bradley, author of *Flyboys*, devotes a chapter titled "Doing the Impossible" to that retaliation and all aspects of the raid, including its genesis. For a complete account of the raid, read Schultz, *The Doolittle Raid.*

The Army Air Force's first plan for the Hump was to supply additional C-47s to China National Aviation Corporation to bring the total to 25 for service on the Hump. (In a remarkable coincidence, it was on December 7, 1941, Pearl Harbor Day, that a CNAC pilot plotted the first Hump air route.) Then a handful of 10th AAF C-47s began modest service to China over northern Burma. But when Japanese ground forces pushed north from Mandalay and conquered Myitkyina, C-47s became vulnerable to Japanese Zeros, and, with a ceiling of only 12,000 feet, could not fly a higher, more northerly route. How many C-47s were shot down is not clear. My interpolation of reported statistics is 11. After 1943, there were only two remaining enemies on the Hump—the terrain and the weather.

The Air Transport Command, given control of the Hump operation in late 1942, brought in C-87s and C-109s, variants of the four-engine B-24 bomber.

CFC: Just a year earlier than the crash of C-46 #996, a C-87 had its own disaster over Tibet. The date was 30 November, 1943. While there are similarities between the two events, there was also a significant difference— the crew of the C-87 bailed out over Tibet and ultimately returned to their base in Jorhat, India. Their near-miraculous recovery is narrated by Sparks and Murcutt in their new book *Lost in Tibet* against an intriguing background of that strange, forbidding culture. The authors drew on books by the pilot, Robert Crozier, and the copilot, Harold McCallum, as well as on other sources.

The weather the C-87 faced on its return flight from China was remarkably similar to what 996 faced a year later. On board the converted bomber was a crew of four plus a GI hitching a ride. According to the report in *Lost in Tibet*, pilot Crozier began an ascent in order to climb over a bank of storm clouds west of the Santsung Range. The C-87 was at 24,000 feet when the storm suddenly struck. Caught in a downdraft, the plane dropped like a stone. A hurricane-speed wind tossed the plane about like a toy. The needle on the direction-finding compass swung wildly, making it impossible to pull in Ft. Hertz, Burma, its next radio checkpoint.

But the C-87 was able, luckily, to establish radio contact with its home field. After receiving a navigational long-count transmission from #270, Jorhat passed on to the crew the heading determined by triangulation—330 degrees! North? Surely, Crozier reasoned, to reach Jorhat they had to fly south. He asked Radio Operator Spencer to double-check. Again Jorhat said 330 degrees. After Spencer was no longer able to raise Jorhat, he reached the tower at Kunming, hundreds of miles to the west, sent out another long count, and received a bearing of 278 degrees.

I wonder what I might have done had I been lost and given a bearing of north! Hump pilots knew that if the wind ever switched from its normal west direction, it would be from the south. No Hump pilot would ever knowingly fly toward the high peaks in the north. Sixty years later, sitting here at my word processor in the comfort of my den, I am certain I would have ignored the bearing given me and turned south. But would I have been so sure of myself then? With their fuel tanks nearly empty, the crew hit the silk, coming down in Tibet, far north of their base in Jorhat, India.

For a while the C-87s and 109s were the only aircraft on the Hump. Then, when the Curtiss twin-engine C-46 came off the production line, 30 were delivered to Karachi in April 1943 and placed in Hump service in Jorhat. Trouble-prone, they were returned to the states for more than 100 modifications and flown back to India in December. Later, four-engine C-54s were added to the southerly route, flying out of Bengal.

Because of the urgent demand for transport aircraft, the C--46 Commando did not have the four-to-five year shakedown that the C-47 enjoyed. Herb Fisher, CBI on-site Curtiss-Wright technical representative, flew research missions on the Hump in an extraordinary effort to eliminate problems. (He had 96 such round-trip flights, the same number, incidentally, as my operational missions. Fisher was much admired and appreciated by Hump pilots.) Fisher recounted (as reported in Flying the Hump *by Ethell and Downie) some of the plane's fault areas and system malfunctions: fuel and hydraulic systems, carburetor shrouds and deicing ability, flight instruments, ignition, cockpit lighting, wing landing lights, cabin heaters, inadequate engine cooling, selectors bypassing fuel from tank to tank, batteries, generators, voltage regulators, fire extinguishers, warning lights, quality of hose connections, auxiliary power unit* failures, nacelle fires. The failures and problems I experienced—all, by the way, after modifications were made—were engine failures, runaway props, wing and carburetor icing, and pesky leaks in the hydraulic system.

Fisher analyzed and solved two serious problems that plagued the Curtiss Commando on the Hump. He determined that the frequent engine fires in flight were caused by deterioration of rubber hose connections and could be solved only by more rigorous inspections and frequent replacements of the hoses. A more puzzling problem was a rash of takeoff crashes on night flights. Flying with many crews, Fisher noticed the tendency of pilots to emulate the airline practice of easing back on power and lowering the nose to save fuel soon after takeoff, trusting their instruments to reveal accurate airspeed and altitude. But these C-46 instruments were not calibrated since they left the factory. An order followed: on night takeoffs, maintain maximum power and 130 mph minimum speed until you reach an altitude of at least 300 feet.

The two-engine C-46 replaced the smaller, dependable, much-loved Douglas C-47 Gooney Bird, (DC-3) as the workhorse of the Hump. The C-46 was designed in 1934 for airline service as the CW-20 and flew first in 1940. It lost out in that market to the Douglas DC-3 and was resurrected by the urgent need for cargo planes at the start of the war. It was the largest twin-engine plane in the world: wingspan 108 ft., length 76 ft. 4 in., height 22 ft., top speed 245 mph, range 1,200 miles, rated ceiling 27,600 ft. It could readily fly over the high peaks of the northerly Hump routes.

But it could not fly over the Hump's 30,000–40,000-ft cumulonimbus thunderheads, as I learned on one scary March 1945 night flight returning from China. Wary of a line of gigantic storms spitting out scary lightning a couple hundred miles ahead in the west, I vowed to fly over them rather than go through them. I got to 24,000 feet but the tops of the evil-looking monsters were still above me. The squall line so huge I could not skirt around it, I bit the bullet and burst right in—a violent roller-coaster ride second only to the perfect storm of January 6 two months earlier. In my foolish effort, I wasted so much fuel climbing we limped back to Chabua with our tanks all but dry.

The 46 carried four tons rather than the C-47's two and a half, and, with a huge, convenient cargo door, was easy to load. Modified for the Army Air Corps, the total production of some 3,000 planes went into military service, most assigned to the Hump.

Ultimately, ATC flew Hump missions mainly out of eight fields in India. C-46s were primarily assigned to a cluster of three fields in northern Assam province—Chabua, Sookerating, and Mohanbari—and to Misamari 170 miles to the southwest.

I still affectionately visualize my C-46 as a smooth, attractive bird with "lines neat and nice," cleaner, less chopped up than the C-47 with its notched nose and tail. The C-46 was a plane to be reckoned with, a handful to fly. Hydraulic assist to the flight controls came off the left engine. When that engine failed, the pilot and copilot together struggled to fly the monster manually. Huge and strong, 100 troops could stand on its wings.

Photo by Ed Gregory
Big and strong, Curtiss C-46 was a beauty, but a handful to fly.

And old Dumbo could take a lot of punishment. In his book
The Hump: The Great Military Airlift of World War II, *Bliss Thorne,*
C-46 Hump pilot, tells about a scary landing he made one night in
China. Because of a cloud covering the whole side of the field, the
tower instructed him to approach and land from the right, not from
the left as normal. Sitting in the right seat, the copilot would have the
best view of the airfield. Bliss therefore gave the copilot the control.
They were already low, way below the peaks surrounding the field.
What Bliss saw was not the strip but fog. "Take it! We're lined up," the
copilot shouted. Between fog and clear patches, Thorne maneuvered
the plane to a landing, striking the runway at the excessive sped of
150 miles an hour. The behemoth bounced 50 feet into the air! No
damage.

I had my own worst landing one night in Myitkyina, Burma.
For some reason, I came in high on the final approach. My copilot
was a veteran Hump pilot who'd been demoted because he'd hit a
wingtip while taxiing. "Put her down," he said. "Don't go around!"
I put her down all right: I dropped the sucker onto the runway in a
three-point stall from 15 feet! No damage.

C-46s were used after the war by the cargo carrier Flying Tiger
Airlines. I've been told they've been flown commercially in Alaska and

Canada as well. "China Doll" and "Tinker Belle," both belonging to the Commemorative Air Force, are the only two Commandos flying stateside. The reader can see a static C-46, #018, at the Air Force Museum at Wright-Patterson Field in Dayton, Ohio. It was retired from USAF service in Panama and brought to the museum in 1972. My logbook slows I flew 018 from Chabua to Kunming on 15 January, 17-18 January and 28-29 January, 1945. Readers who visit the Air Force Academy in Colorado Springs can see a stunning bronze 1/6 scale model of a C-46, displayed in the Honor Court with other war birds mounted there to make WWII come alive for cadets. Members of the CBI Hump Pilots Association presented the beautiful bird to the Academy during HPA's 2004 reunion in Denver.

An anonymous pilot stationed in Sookerating wrote a poetic lament about the C-46, variously dubbed Plumber's Nightmare, Flying Coffin, Old Dumbo. It's taken from A Small Book About Sook.

The Mistake

Maybe I'm wrong in telling you this,
But blueprints and pilots don't mix.
'Cause someone got a bug up his ass
And designed the C-46.

It's a Curtiss mistake or a lunatic's dream—
Sure those lines are neat and nice,
But who gives a damn for those beautiful lines
When you hit a cloudful of ice?

They say it's made to soar like a bird.
Yeah, those blueprints talk a sweet dish.
But that stuff was made for magazines,
For this ship acts more like a fish.

They say it's the largest twin-engine ship
And that you couldn't ask for more.
But ask the guy who's been sweatin' a few:
He'll tell you it ought to have four.
They'll tear it apart and build it again.
They'll swear it's licked (the designer thinks).

So you'll take it up and try it again,
And you'll find the Commando still stinks.

When things go wrong and that Hump looks near
And you feel kinda close to heaven,
Then you'll curse the ship for the mess you're in
And pray for a C-47.

In the beginning, Hump operations were conducted only in daytime. As other models were brought in to supplement the C-47s, round-the-clock flying became the norm and weather was not to be considered in dispatching flights. Col Thomas Hardin, the new Hump Commander, held the Weather Service in low regard. He decreed, "There is no weather on the Hump." Not to be outdone as a macho man, Hardin's successor, Gen William Tunner, later commander of the Berlin Airlift, amended the decree slightly: "The Hump is never closed."

The three contenders for the Hump's tonnage—Stilwell, Chennault, and Chiang Kai-shek—quarreled bitterly over priorities. Tonnage increased gradually, then dramatically. Totally, from 1942 through 1945 the Hump operation delivered 720,000 tons of cargo to southwest China in 167,000 flights. At the end of the war, ATC Hump aircraft inventory included 330 C-46s, 167 C-47s, and 132 C-54s, C-87s, and C-109s. At war's end, 600 ATC transport planes landed in China every day—this only 40 years after the Wright Brothers' first flight!

On 1 August 1945 I pulled the duty of tower-officer-of-the-day at Chabua. It was a big day—Army Air Force Day. Rather than accepting General Arnold's recommendation that all commands celebrate by having parades or open houses, General Tunner, the Hump Commander, took a different tack. August 1 would be a day of work as usual on the Hump. And what a day of work. His goal: break the existing one-day tonnage record. It worked. At the end of the 24-hour day, the Command had flown 1,118 round-trips, a plane crossing the Hump every minute and twelve seconds, over 5,000 tons carried. Tunner himself flew three round-trips.

I agreed with General Tunner that so close to Japan and in backwater venues, parades would be inappropriate. But I didn't think

much at all of his bravado idea—too much hoopla, too theatrical. Mine
not to reason why. But who knows? Perhaps a motivation like this was
in the general's memory bank three years later when he commanded
the Berlin Airlift so brilliantly.

The CBI was primarily a British and Chinese ground theater;
for the U.S. it was primarily an air theater. The Air Transport
Command was the largest command. Other non-tactical air
commands—Troop Carrier, Combat Cargo, Air Commandos, and
China National Aviation Corporation—delivered supplies and troops
throughout the theater. ATC pilots based in India who flew to China
were the basic Hump pilots. Other ATC pilots were stationed in
China to deliver Hump supplies to Burma across the corners of the
Hump, to other fields around China, and at times to fly supplies and
Chinese troops to India. Troop Carrier and Combat Cargo C-47s,
most based in India, had the scary assignment of supplying Merrill's
Marauders and Wingate's Chindits behind enemy lines in Burma, at
times landing on improvised runways, at times discharging parachuted
or free-fall packages kicked out by "cargo kickers." While their flights
were mainly across the corners of the Hump, they made occasional
full Hump trips on the southerly route.

In addition to cargo units, tactical air units were active against
the enemy in the CBI—10th Air Force, 14th Air Force, 20th Air
Force with its B-29s, Royal Air Force, Royal Canadian Air Force,
and other fighter and bomber groups and squadrons. Some U.S.
units were both tactical and non-tactical. Gus Forsman, a friend from
Aviation Cadets, flew B-24s with the 7th Bomb Group, 9th Squadron
out of Tezpur, India. When there were no longer enemy targets to
bomb within range of the airplane, the squadron was assigned to haul
gasoline to China over the Hump. (See his story on pages 99 – 101 of
my Tales of the Himalayas.)

Unlike the well-known personalities of the CBI, and unlike
hot-shot fighter and bomber pilots, Hump pilots and crew were
anything but glamorous. The 1978 Time-Life WWII book China-
Burma-India referred to us as "swash-buckling pilots of the China
Wing of the ATC, "living like dogs, and flying like fiends, halting
only for weather so bad that—as the saying went—even the birds were
grounded." We did not live like dogs, we were not flying fiends, but

yes, the weather never stopped us. But we were anything but "swash-buckling." We were long-haul truck drivers, eager to put in our time on the road and go home.

But the First Commando Group might deserve the epithet "Swash-buckling." A diversified organization commanded by Colonels Phil Cochran and John Alison, the group had its own air force—P-51s, B-25s, C-47s, L-5s, and TG-5 gliders. "Operation Thursday" on March 5, 1944, was its biggest glider mission—54 gliders bound for "Broadway" in Burma at night behind enemy lines. Seventeen didn't make it. Cochran, incidentally, was the model for Flip Cockran in the old comic strip "Terry and the Pirates." Alison, an early C-40 fighter pilot in China, acquired a reputation as one of best pilots in the Army Air Force.

CFC: Frank Wenrich, WWII glider-pilot friend from Reading, PA volunteered for the "Operation Thursday" mission. I hold a restricted definition of war hero, but Frank qualifies. (Read his story in my *Tales of the Himalayas*.)

^^^

Looking back on my year in the CBI, I realize how sheltered, how socially impoverished my life there was. Life on the base was socially dull, mind-numbingly dull. On my 96 round-trip flights to China (occasionally to Burma) I was never once allowed off base to visit a city or town. I never flew into any of the dozen ATC fields in India other than my own or into the ATC bases in China other than four to which I was at times dispatched.

I was amazed to read how many commands, organizations, and units operated in the China-Burma-India theater—122! Of course we were all there to keep China in the war. On the ground the United States had only a few thousand tactical troops—Merrill's Marauders, the OSS, and Stilwell's advisers to the Chinese Army. There were other thousands of U.S. troops who served in non-AAF units on the ground—road-builders on the Ledo Road, engineers, pipe-line and telephone line workers, radio repair units, engineers, truck drivers on the Burma Road, heavy equipment units, service units, and more.

^^^

How will history judge the CBI and the Hump? The Hump's primary purpose, to supply China to keep her in the war, was a clear success. The word going around the Hump was that much of what we delivered was stolen by warlords. If that was true, and I believe it was, many Americans lost their lives needlessly.

A second purpose of the Hump, to hold bases in eastern China for the ultimate invasion of Japan, was obviated when the Enola Gay dropped history's first atom bomb. But the third purpose, tying up a million Japanese troops, was successful. One thing is certain. The Hump demonstrated the feasibility of supplying troops or nations by air. It was the precursor of airlifts in Korea and of course the famous Berlin Airlift.

White and Jacoby sum up the China-Burma-India operation succinctly. "The sole reason for the existence of this theater was to keep China in the war....Almost a quarter million Americans were assigned to this task; billions of dollars were spent; thousands of lives were lost. It was an essential mission. What was accomplished here was awarded less recognition, less support, less encouragement, than any other phase of America's war effort."

Airman's Blood Chit

Downed C-B-I airmen displayed a blood chit inside their flight jackets in order to communicate with Chinese or Burmese natives. The message is: "Military friend, I am in the American Air Force. I came to China to help fight the Japanese. Please give me help and also notify our Allies. The United States Government thanks you."

Chapter 6

Negotiating with China

The Joint POW/MIA Account Command in Hawaii learns about MIAs from America's wars from military records, outside researchers, the national archives, foreign depositories, veterans, historians, amateur researchers, and families of MIAs. The Command first creates an incident file of histories of the conflict, archival documents from each service branch, official correspondence, maps, photographs, unit histories, military medical and personnel records. Then analysts provide the operations and laboratory sections with information about the loss. After obtaining permission to proceed to the country where the MIA mission will be undertaken, an investigative or recovery team is deployed to the site. (The 2002 Rouse team that recovered the remains of a 4-man C-46 crew near Langko in Tibet also investigated the Damnya crash site for the 2004 excavation/recovery that is the subject of this book.)

When the Central Identification Laboratory team had gone into Southeast Asia on recovery missions, they worked with the Joint Task Force—Full Accounting, a command set up for recovery from the Vietnam War. The Lab conducted missions worldwide as well. Since Capt Kent's last mission to Vietnam, the 30-year-old CILHI merged with the 11-year-old Joint Task Force to form JPAC.

To obtain permission of the People's Republic of China for the mission, in early February 2004 Team Leader Kent and Mrs. Nasarenko, deputy for policy, flew to Beijing. They were joined in the negotiations by three members of the U.S. Defense Attache Office at the Embassy there—Mick Riva, Wes Andrews, Ms. Heidi Gomez, and by two members of the Defense POW/MIA Personnel—Lt Col Mark Franklin and Commander James Wong. Maj Riva, USMC from South Florida, a foreign affairs officer who speaks fluent Chinese, was their linguist. Capt Kent's superior, Lt Col Dave Buckingham, in charge of negotiations for two previous China missions, led the discussions for the U.S. delegation. When he was tasked by name to report to Iraq, Capt Kent moved up as chief negotiator for discussions to follow in Lhasa, Tibet. For the protocol session in Beijing, JPAC had already forwarded discussion points to the Chinese representatives, leading to relaxed and pleasant exchanges.

The following day, 8 February, the U.S. representatives, escorted by Majors Riva and Andrews, left for Lhasa, since 1951 capital of the Tibet Autonomous Region of China, for operational/logistical assessment meetings. The party stayed overnight in Chengdu, China, meeting with U.S. Consulate officials and the Consul General, Jeff Moon, at his home for dinner. Team members left Chengdu the next morning, arriving in Lhasa at 3:30 in the afternoon, and were escorted to the Lhasa Hotel. Sessions began the following day.

Officials from the PRC included two representatives from the U.S. Affairs Division, Department of North American and Oceania Affairs—Mr. Xu Chaoyou, Deputy Director, and Mr. Mu Zhouqing, Interpreter. Representatives of TAR included Mr. Ju Jianhu, Deputy Director-General; Mr. Targa, Director of TAR Foreign Affairs Office and Tibetan Team Leader; Mr. Wangla, Financial Director; and Mr. Yen Shuming.

The word *negotiations* can connote harsh, adversarial meetings between parties working on a labor agreement or governments signing treaties. Tension was not the tone of these sessions. Both sides desired the goodwill of the other—the U.S. to pursue its long-standing tradition of retrieving remains of MIAs, China to enhance its international image and to further social and economic change and international trade. The American delegates happily sported the Tibetan stoles (hadas) given them as gifts of welcome.

CFC: CBI friends who have returned to China as tourists tell me the people of Kunming and Yunnan Province in southwest China are effusive in their gratitude for the Flying Tigers and the Hump airlift in what they call the "War Against Fascism."

Every June in my hometown of Reading, PA, the Mid Atlantic Air Museum holds its WWII Weekend, well-known by aviation and history buffs. At my CBI/Hump booth in the hangar last year a Chinese-American man stopped to buy my books and to thank me—a dozen "thank-you's" in two minutes—for my service flying the Hump.

U.S. and Chinese negotiators at the Foreign Affairs Office in Lhasa, Capital of the Tibetan Autonomous Region. The Americans are wearing their "hadas", gifts of friendship from their hosts, (left to right) Dung Yu, Shen Pang, Ju Jiznhua, Xu Chaoyou, Capt. Kent, Mrs. Nasarenko, Mr. Targa, Maj. Riva, Maj. Andrews

Maj Riva opened the Lhasa conference on behalf of the U.S. Ambassador and Defense Attache, thanking the PRC officials for their hospitality, saying he looked forward to productive sessions. Before he introduced Capt Kent as the U.S. team leader, he made an official request regarding safety. He asked that Mr. Targa participate in the upcoming 2004 mission. Targa, a former athlete and PRC team leader in the 2002 mission, is highly regarded by the American delegation.

On behalf of Maj Gen W. Montague Winfield, commander of JPAC, as well as families of U.S. service members still missing from WWII and veterans who served with them, Capt Kent expressed his appreciation for the Chinese willingness to assist in the recovery. He stated that Tibetan officials have a great reputation as a result of the support they provided to the U.S. 2002 team. "Our Team 2004," Capt Kent said, "is eagerly looking forward to coming here for this mission." He noted that the 14-member team has been identified and included an anthropologist, a physician, medics, linguists, mortuary specialists, mountaineers, and a photographer. He said one of his goals was to leave Tibet with a detailed schedule, a budget plan, and an opportunity to inspect equipment left in Lhasa after the 2002 mission. He concluded his opening remarks by noting that safety was the number one concern, especially important because the Damyna site is considered far more difficult to excavate than the 2002 Langko site.

Mr. Ju introduced members of the PRC delegation and Mr. Targa as an expert on weather on the high plateau. He said they would take the U.S. request to have Mr. Targa participate into full consideration, but it was not certain Mr. Targa would be able to participate. He assured Maj Riva that a very experienced person would be chosen as guide. Maj Riva stated that his intent was not to interfere with the composition of the Tibetan team but out of concern for safety.

Capt Kent addressed the problem of evacuating a person injured in the mission. Because of the rugged terrain and the isolation of the excavation site, an evacuation would be made by ground until reaching Bayi. The injured would be carried to Damnya then transported by 4x4 vehicle to Bayi People's Hospital. An international SOS aircraft out of the Lhasa Airport would then fly the injured to an appropriate medical facility. The team physician and two medical corpsmen specializing in high altitude operations and equipped with a Class VIII medical package would supervise the evacuation and care for the injured.

Capt Kent next discussed communications, vital on all JPAC missions and a top priority of Gen Winfield in order to assure the safety of his teams. Capt Kent listed the systems:

1. Iridium phones
2. INMARSAT
3. HF radio
4. Motorola hand-held radios
5. Motorola Talk-about
6. Cellular phones

Capt Kent then proposed an arrival and departure schedule for the mission. The JPAC team would arrive in Beijing on 30 July, travel to Lhasa on 6 August, conduct the excavation from 27 August through 9 October, return to Lhasa and on to Beijing, depart China for Hawaii on 27 October. In response, the Tibetan delegation requested an adjustment to Capt Kent's proposed timeline, asking for the U.S. team to arrive late in August rather than earlier. His schedule was based on the 2002 mission. The later arrival would avoid the rainy season, when roads are impassable, the Tibetan delegation said. After examining the plan, JPAC stated that although the mission could perhaps complete its accounting in as few as five days, the U.S. plan allowed for a worst-case-scenario excavation lasting as long as 45 days.

Mr. Ju stated his opinion that it was not necessary or practicable for the U.S. team to remain in Lhasa for 10 days, saying two days would be sufficient for acclimatization. Capt Kent explained that during this period the team would conduct light exercise then progress to hiking to 15,500 feet for acclimatization to conduct the mission and stay in safe proximity of an airfield in the event of an emergency. Capt Kent provided the following schedule:

Day 1   Arrive Lhasa (elevation 12,500 feet), Rest
Day 2   Rest, Sight-seeing, Light exercise
Day 3   Walking, Light exercise, Sight-seeing, Rest
Day 4   Two-hour hike with no elevation gain
Day 5   Two-to-three hour hike to an elevation of 14,000 feet
Day 6   Medical assessment, Sight-seeing, Rest
Day 7   Hike to 15,500 feet, camp at 14,000 feet
Day 8   Return to Lhasa, Rest
Day 9   Medical evaluation, Final equipment preparations
Day 10 Depart Lhasa for excavation site

Mr. Ju said the altitude of Lhasa is significantly lower than the altitude at the crash site. Capt Kent responded that the JPAC concern was not about that difference but rather the difference between the sea-level elevation of Hawaii and the mountain elevation of Tibet, averaging 12,000 feet. The physician on the 2002 mission had strongly recommended a 10-day adjustment period, Capt Kent added. He asked that if a 10-day period is not acceptable, the Tibetan delegation consider something longer than two days.

Mr. Ju said there were no mountains near Lhasa as high as those proposed by Capt Kent in his schedule. He asked Capt Kent to consider going to a suburb of Lhasa for part of the acclimatization process. Mr. Lu explained there is a mountain about 90 km from Lhasa with a height of 4,000 to 5,000 meters. He added there would be an important festival in Lhasa during the proposed time, and he was concerned about having the U.S. team in Lhasa then, adding that there would not be enough PRC officials available to support the U.S. team during this period.

Capt Kent said the suggested mountain sounded acceptable. Saying he could adjust the time in order for the team to be less intrusive during the festival, he nevertheless stated that seven days would be the minimum acceptable time for acclimatization. He agreed to the date of 14 August for the U.S. team to arrive in Lhasa.

Mr. Ju said he understood it was impossible to give an exact completion date for the mission. He agreed to allow the U.S. team to stay as long as necessary to get the job done. He added, however, that because of dangerous weather conditions, the team would not be allowed to remain on the mountain in October. He asked Capt Kent to give his word that he would pull his team off the mountain should safety concerns arise. Stating that safety was also his number one concern, Capt Kent agreed, saying he would consult with his team leadership as well as with leaders of the Tibetan team to make a joint decision about continuing the mission if the weather turned bad. The two sides agreed to a 30-day excavation window and a 7-day acclimatization period in Lhasa.

The parties agreed on the following mission schedule:

14 AUG	**U.S. team arrives Lhasa.**
15 – 21 AUG	**Equipment preparations,** acclimatization, exercise hikes. The team will make two high hikes, one to 14,000 feet, one to 15,500. Team

	members will exercise and walk extensively throughout Lhasa.
22 AUG	**U.S. and PRC teams depart Lhasa** for Lingzhi Prefecture
23 AUG	**Team meeting with officials** of prefecture
24 AUG	**Training for PRC workers** with U.S. team
25 AUG	**Move to Minlin County**
26 AUG	**Contact with departments** concerned with labor and pack animals
27 AUG	**Depart for Dannaing Twp. by vehicle** Hike toward Danniang Mt. along DouQiong Ravine, Base Camp 1
28 AUG	**Cross Dannaing Mt.; arrive Base** Camp 2, Duorebange
29 AUG	**Hike along mountain toward Base** Camp 3, Dangjicuo
30 AUG	**Arrive at excavation site; set up camp**
31 AUG – 01 OCT	**Conduct excavation mission**
02- 05 OCT	**Depart site for Danniang Twp.**
06 OCT	**Arrive Minlin County**
07 OCT	**Return to Lingzhi Prefecture**
08 OCT	**Rest in Lingzhi Prefecture**
09 OCT	**Return to Lhasa**
10 OCT	**Conduct technical processing of** materials recovered at site. (Documentation and certification must be accomplished to remove human remains and artifacts from China. Team leader, along with U.S. Embassy representatives, will
11 OCT	coordinate with PRC officials.) **Meet with officials in Lhasa for** debriefing
12 OCT	**Depart Lhasa for Beijing**

Capt Kent requested assurance from the Tibetan delegation that the site remain undisturbed in order to assure its integrity for excavation and that U.S. team be able to leave Tibet with any and all evidence found. The TAR delegation assured him they had no issue with these matters.

Following the operational agreement, the Tibetan representatives presented a budget proposal based on the 2002 agreement and excavation period, with increases in wages for laborers for the 2004 mission. Noting that much of the equipment requested was purchased for and used in the 2002 mission and remained the property of the U.S. Government, Capt Kent requested permission to inspect that equipment. Negotiations were suspended while JPAC made the inspection at the Ministry of Foreign Affairs compound.

All equipment was either unserviceable or unaccounted for. Capt Kent expressed his concern for accountability of such items and informed Mr. Targa he intended to conduct a before-and-after inventory of all equipment, including vehicles, and require that all equipment be properly stored for use in further operations in Tibet. Mr. Targa agreed.

Budget discussions resumed. JPAC agreed to requests for purchases, but informed TAR delegates that accountability would be strictly enforced. It was agreed that Health and Medical Care fees, as well as compensation for lost pack animals, would be handled by the team leaders of both parties on a case-by-case basis at the end of the mission. The day's negotiations were then adjourned.

The parties met for dinner. To the delight of Maj Riva and Capt Kent, at the dinner Mr. Targa introduced himself as TAR Team Leader for the mission. The JPAC team congratulated him and expressed confidence he would do a spectacular job, as he had on the 2002 mission.

Discussions reconvened at 0930 hours the next day, 10 February. Items included in the final compensation agreement based on a 30-day excavation included:

1. Technological equipment
2. Basic equipment
3. Food and utensils

4. Personal equipment
5. Per diem living costs
6. Local labor and pack animals
7. Business trips subsidies
8. Transportation
9. Emergency contingency fee
10. Establishment of joint office

The U.S. and PRC delegations agreed on the following financial arrangements:

1. The official exchange rate for all financial transactions will be 8.265 Chinese Yuan per 1.00 U.S. Dollar.

2. Payment for the operation will be made in two installments, the advance payment no later than 15 June, the final payment at the end of the mission.

3. The advance payment will cover the cost of items necessary for purchase in advance of the arrival of the U.S. team.

4. Costs requiring determination of total number of mission days, labor, pack animals, accommodations, and emergency fees will be settled at the conclusion of the mission.

5. Reimbursement of 50,000 CYN ($6049.61) per pack animal lost during the mission.

6. Officials in Lhasa will provide to the U.S. Embassy representative a bank name and account number prior to 15 June 2004.

7. The U.S. Embassy representative will accomplish all financial transactions.

Capt Kent informed the PRC that JPAC would establish a liaison office in Beijing to coordinate activities associated with conducting missions in China and the Democratic Republic of Korea from April to October. In addition, there will be a joint coordinating office in Lhasa staffed by a JPAC or U.S. Embassy representatives as well as a PRC official.

The talks concluded with Capt Kent and Maj Riva thanking the PRC officials for their cooperation in reaching agreements. Mr. Ju stated he was looking forward to equal success in 2004 as was accomplished in 2002. Mr. Xu complimented Capt Kent on his attention to detail and said he was confident the team would find success on the mountain.

After exchanging further pleasantries with their counterparts, the U.S. delegation departed Lhasa for Beijing that afternoon. Members agreed that the Chinese and TAR personnel provided complete support in planning and expressed their desire for a first-rate humanitarian mission and their desire to do so in future missions.

Relaxing after the two-day negotiating conference, Capt Kent said he was excited and pleased to take the lead in the delegation. He felt it was a big advantage for the team leader to also be the leader of the negotiations. He was gratified at dinner one night to be pulled aside by Mr. Targa, who told him how dedicated he would be to the mission. "That," Captain Kent said, "was good enough for me."

Chapter 7

Recovery Leader/Mortuary Affairs Specialists

D r. Andrew Tyrell, forensic anthropologist of London, England, was appointed Recovery Leader for the Damnya mission. His will be job number 1 when the team reaches the crash site.

Andy had heard about the Central Identification Laboratory in Hawaii (CILHI) while he was completing his doctoral studies at the University of Sheffield, England, in 1999. He applied to work for the lab but discovered that employment was available only to American citizens. He went to work as Human Rights investigator for non-governmental organizations in Yugoslavia for a year. Then he learned from a CILHI friend of a new fellowship program that did not require American citizenship. He applied, got the position, and came to Hawaii to work as a researcher for CILHI for three years. Last year CILHI (since merged into JPAC) made Andy permanent; he was thrilled to be put on as an MIA recovery anthropologist.

As a schoolboy, Andy was lucky to have a teacher who started a climbing club, giving up weekends to take a truckload of boys to Wales and, as the boys grew older, to the Alps. Later young Andy got to run his own mountaineering club and organize his own expeditions. He remains an avid climber. To become an anthropologist for JPAC was a dream fulfilled.

His first MIA mission was to Laos—no mountains to climb there! But in recovering C-46 Curtiss Commandos, he has come full circle, for the crash excavated in Laos was also of a C-46. The jungle of Laos was rough, as were the jungles of Vietnam and Burma he visited in later missions. But they paled, he said, in comparison with the jungles of Papua New Guinea, where he went on his last mission to do a series of investigations for future recoveries. Still, he said, the jungles of Burma are a scary if beautiful sight from the air. He recalled the cryptic question of a helicopter pilot as Andy prepared to bail out. "You sure?" he asked. Within a few minutes, Andy was neck-high in jungle grass.

In addition to missions in Burma, Laos, and Papua New Guinea, he has been on MIA excavations in Luxemburg, France, Belgium, and Germany. But the mission to the Himalayan Mountains of Tibet, the most dangerous ever, will outshine them all, he said.

The role of recovery leader begins, Andy explained, when the team reaches the crash. His first responsibility is to lay out the total site. "The Tibet 2004 site will be particularly challenging," he said, "because the plane crashed near the top of a cliff and the wreckage lies over a wide area on a steep slope layered in rocks and boulders. Photographs from a 2002 investigative mission showed a tight focus of wreckage and material evidence at the top of the slope as well as pieces of aircraft 1,000 feet below.

"On this recovery, as in so many others," Andy said, "I was moved by the tremendous bad luck of a crew who crashed less than 100 meters below a ridge line. It is extremely gratifying to be engaged in work that ensures that sacrifices of past generations are not forgotten."

Among an anthropologist's other duties are developing a strategy for excavating the site, managing evidence, and taking care of material and artifacts recovered. MIA anthropologists are civilians, providing a level of independence in making identifications. Although he supposed a bit of a military vs. civilian culture could exist, he and Geoff, like Lewis and Clark, are a congenial and effective team. "Geoff has a good personality and is very easy to get along with."

Andy is 34, married, has a house in Hawaii but is still a British citizen. He enjoys reading books, painting, art appreciation, and playing the guitar. "People who hear me play," he said wryly, "find it entirely believable that I'm self-taught."

ᐱᐱᐱ

Three team members—Sergeants Swam, Harris, and Castro—are specialists in Mortuary Affairs. JPAC in Hawaii handles MIAs missing and presumed dead. The "real world" division of MA, based in Ft Lee, Virginia, locates, identifies, recovers, and prepares remains of casualties of current wars. On the Tibet 2004 mission, all three MAs will work hand-in-hand with Anthropologist Tyrell in the recovery process—including setting up the site, preparing wet screens or dry screens, determining in advance the recovery equipment needed, and taking charge of equipment.

 **Staff Sergeant Mike Harris** began our interview with a cheery greeting. "Living in Hawaii is awesome. You can't do much better than this," he said. "Six years here, two at Schofield Barracks, four at Hickam—I'm practically a native." Mike was born in San Angelo, Texas, in 1971, a Navy brat whose father moved a lot, mostly from Jacksonville to Memphis and back several times.

Mike had some college and is working on a degree. He entered military service at Memphis in 1991, his first job a single-channel radio operator. It was at his first station in Fort Riley, Kansas, that he read in *Soldier's Magazine* about the specialty of Mortuary Affairs. Wanting to escape a boring job, at reenlist time he applied for MA and made it. He has been on missions to Vietnam, Laos, Papua New Guinea, and Germany, some multiple times. He's had three to five missions a year, upwards of 20 in all.

He was on the Tibet 2002 mission. "Those poor guys flew smack into the face of the mountain and just slid down," he said. "The wrecked plane was pretty much intact, much more so than some of the jets we recovered elsewhere traveling at Mock Whatever. The 2004 Damnya site looks like a bigger site, more spread out."

The 2002 team hit pay dirt, Mike said. Not only did they have a good recovery at the prime site, they also sent out an investigative team that confirmed the Damnya site. Like the earlier Tibet excavation, this one will be physically demanding, he said. Unlike most of the team, he confessed that climbing is not in his blood. "I wouldn't do it for fun on weekends," he added.

"The Alaska training was a smoker," he said, "tougher, actually, than my last Vietnam mission. The Northern Warfare Training Center did a really good job with us."

Mike looks forward to working again with Sergeant Swam, from whom he learned a lot, he said. He hopes on some future mission he will make as exciting a discovery as he did in a marshy, muddy area near Lake Miola in Papua New Guinea. He was shocked to find a wallet that had been sealed solid, allowing no new water to get into it. "The pictures in the wallet were perfect. Awesome!"

The "Repate" ceremonies in Hawaii are inspiring, he said. As the remains in flag-draped coffins are taken off the plane, the company, standing in formation, salutes and renders honors. Civilians who work for JPAC are there, as are news crews, sometimes family members and veterans organizations.

Mike is married. He and his wife have an 8-year-old daughter, Kane. He acknowledged it's hard to be away from them, especially when they know he's working in a dangerous area. "But I look on my job as an honor, as a debt, to bring these guys home and give their families closure," he said. "The respect is not just to those who died but to all our veterans. All paid a price. A message we convey to our recruits is this—these are our fallen comrades, and we don't forget them."

Mike has been a rugby player for nine years in the men's league in Hawaii. Being away on missions of course cuts into practice time. But more than rugby, more than anything else, he enjoys family time.

^^^

 **Sergeant Albert Castro,** at 37 a "fairly old soldier," as he put it, came into the service in a late career move. Bachelor's degree from Cal Poly Pomona in 1992 and also a culinary arts graduate, Al worked in the food/restaurant business for 10 years, mainly in California, with some time in Europe. He does not come from a military family; he can't recall how the military got his attention.

Before burning out and losing his passion for cooking, he wanted to try something new. He was single, and his savings invested, he'd see if he could put in some time in the military, perhaps take advantage of the GI bill in pursuing a master's and doctor's in food science.

Al was born in Newport Beach, California, and grew up in Costa Mesa. He joined the military at Fort Lee, Virginia, when he was 32. After a year and a half he made sergeant; then, as a 92 Mike (Mortuary Affairs Specialty), he was sent to CILHI in Hawaii as his second duty station. The laboratory has since merged with JPAC. Coming up on six years, he intends to reenlist for another three-year term. If all goes well, he'll have no problem opting for 20 years.

When Al enlisted, he had no idea he'd be part of an MIA recovery team. He enjoys the work. He got himself back into good physical condition, he's again motivated to do new things, and he's getting a liberal education about world cultures, especially the cultures of Southeast Asia. He's been there 14 times. He recalled a childhood incident in California when, in fourth grade in the post-Vietnam era, his teacher introduced a Vietnamese mother and her daughter who would become a classmate. It was neat, he said, later in life, to experience their culture and to better understand the people of the world. "The best thing," he said, "is to try to get along and have more encounters on the friendly level."

His philosophy is grounded in 15 MIA missions since 1 October 2000. His two most memorable missions were one in Laos and one in Vietnam. A plane had crashed into the side of a mountain in Laos. The team recovered no remains but found a significant personal effect, a wedding ring inscribed with the pilot's initials as well as his wife's. In the memorable Vietnam mission, in the province called Namdinh, the team had tough work. The ground and sand of the site near the ocean were saturated with aviation fuel. The team installed steel plates and beams. The mission turned out to be highly labor intensive, the team digging down seven and a half meters to screen for bone and artifacts. The team found a lot of human remains, as well as ID cards. He will never forget working every day in that difficult site, gasoline fumes always present, he said.

Al looks forward to the Tibet mission. He believes the mix of services on the teams is a plus, and he's pleased to be associated with so strong and intelligent a group. This team seems especially close, he feels, the mountain training in Alaska having yielded first-class morale. "Harris and I work in the same squad," he said, "handing things off to each other, at the end of the day feeling good about the work." All team members are pretty much the same, regardless of rank, he said. We all pretty much dance to the tune of the anthropologist, he added.

Al's avocations are horticulture and tennis. "There aren't many tennis players in the unit, but I find matches outside the unit. And one big plus—it's summer here every day."

Connections

I see two connections to Sergeant Castro—our interest in education and world cultures, and our love of tennis. He told me his father is 79 and is still playing. I'm 84 and playing four times a week, doubles of course. His father and I go back to the years of the Jack Kramer wooden racket, kept from bending when not in use by a wooden press tightened with butterfly screws.

Chapter 8

Briefing the General

JFA (04-03CH)
10 AUG – 17 OCT 04

IRDB #3

In early June, Capt Kent and his support staff briefed the JPAC Commander, Maj Gen W. Montague Winfred, and his staff on Tibet Mission 04-3CH, scheduled for August through 17 October at site number CH-00628 in Dymnya Township, Milin County, Tibet Autonomous Region of the People's Republic of China. Purpose of the mission is to recover remains and artifacts of three US crewmen of MACR 9675, a C-46 aircraft that crashed on November 3, 1944.

MACR 9675

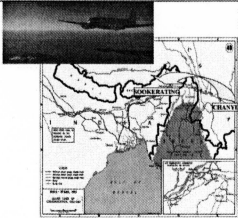

- The "Hump" 1942-1945
- Resupply Allied Forces in China by Air after Japanese forces cut the "Burma Road"
- 14 Airbases in India; 4 in China
- Cargo Airplanes (C46s, C47s and others) flew around the clock and in all conditions
- 600 aircraft and 1000 men were lost

- November 1944, C46 Commando departed Chanyi to head back to home station of Sookerating (1337ª AAFBU)
- "Mayday"; Bearing indicated NE of Sookerating
- Unknown as to cause of crash

- 3 Member Crew BNR

Communication Support

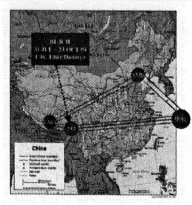

Command
Operational C2 is from the Team to the COC at JPAC

SIGNAL
Team in Field (Redundant Communications)
- 2 Inmarsat (w/ solar charger and high capacity batteries)
- 2 Iridium to All
- 2 Iridium pagers
- 5 Talkabouts
- CF-29 Laptop (Sourced from SEA or new purchase)

Embassy LNO stationed in Lhasa,
- SATCOM
- Cell phone
- Land-line capability

	Inmarsat
	Iridium
	WW cell phone
	LandLine
	Email

Using power-point slides, Capt Kent illustrated the:

✓ Planning timetable, including the tasking of the Northern Warfare Training Center for mountain training, publishing of Warning Orders and Operations Orders, mountain training in Alaska, confirmation brief, deployment activities, and mission execution

✓ Description of site—discovered by Tibetan hunters in 1999, investigated by team from the 2002 CILHI Tibet mission. Wreckage and material correlated by the Rouse investigative party to known loss of a C-46. Life-support items photographed and left in place

✓ Recovery team—names and assignments

✓ Current threat—terrorist threat low, crime threat low

✓ Weather pattern—Tibet transitioning from summer Low to winter High, decreasing moisture and rain, snow in higher elevations approximately five days in October, ceilings average 3,000 feet, mean minimum temperature 50 F in August, 36 F in October

✓ Movement capability—when dry, movement good on plains, wide valleys and salt flats; when wet, movement confined to areas of coarse-grained soils and established routes

✓ Operation in six phases—1) pre-deployment (including team training in Oahu and Alaska), 2) deployment, 3) training and acclimatization in Tibet, 4) movement to crash site and establishing of site, 5) movement to Beijing, 6) redeployment

✓ Flight plan—scheduled in military C-17 and commercial aircraft for cargo and passengers in deployment and redeployment phases

✓ Mission timetable—from arrival in Tibet on 10 August through meetings and final coordination, equipment preparations, acclimatization, procuring local workers and pack animals, training of workers, movement to site, establishing bases, conducting excavation and recovery of remains, returning to Lhasa, technical processing of materials recovered, de-briefing of Embassy officials on 13-17 October

Time Distance Factors

Route to Damnya Crash Site from Village

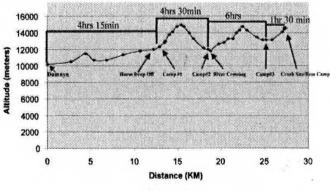

Route and Site Overview

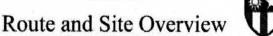

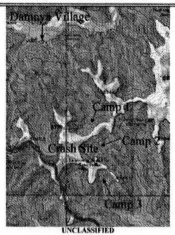

✓ Movements to camps—to Camp 1 (4 hrs 15 min, 8.3 miles, climb and camp at 12,300 feet); to Camp 2 (4 hrs 30 min, climb to 14,800 feet and camp at 12,000 feet); to Camp 3 (6 hrs 3.4 miles, climb to 14, 700 feet and camp at 12, 750 feet); to crash site and final camp (1 hr 30 min, 1.25 miles, climb to 14,300 feet, camp there

✓ Recovery Leader's assessment—aircraft equipment but no remains have been seen on surface of site; wreckage scattered over large area and has become partially incorporated into unconsolidated breccia that lines hanging corrie; site specifically correlated using tail number on vertical stabilizer; post-depositional processes, including scavenging, gravitational and alluvial transport mechanisms, and a CILHI investigation that disturbed the site since incident.

✓ Excavation strategy presented in Recovery Leader's assessment—a mixture of stratigraphic and block excavation and contemporaneous strata; strategy is to complete units individually with completed units used as location for spoil pile of neighboring units to minimize transportation of excavated sediments; excavation arduous, consisting mostly of moving overlying clasts of breccia (limited, if any, local labor available); screening requirements likely minimal, but a few small, individual screening tables will be constructed pre-deployment, disassembled for transport and rebuilt on site.

✓ Risk assessment of Damnya site—judged medium overall, with foot movement in mountains high and medevac time extra high because of time to airfield (nine plus hours)

✓ Risk mitigation—high risk of foot movement mitigated by physical training, personnel selection based on physical ability/experience, rest breaks, fixed ropes emplaced by mountaineers ahead of main body, three experienced medics, specialized mountain training in Alaska, some team members from 2002 Tibet mission; extra high risk of medevac time mitigated by experienced medics, specialized training, redundant satellite communications, liaison in Lhasa, airport in Lhasa; preparation for altitude—increase sleeping altitude by 1,000 feet a night above 10,000; climb high, sleep low; diet, exercise, attitude, medical kit

✓ Medevac—International SOS (ISOS) Singapore and/ or Lhasa Liaison Officer notified, movement-by-foot to Damnya village, movement by vehicle to Bayi or, if required, Lhasa, transfer to Lhasa airport, ISOS Beijing most probable transfer location, fixed-wing ISOS charter (ICU capable) out of Beijing.

✓ Potential medical risks—mild to moderate, Acute Mountain Sickness/Hace, traveler's diarrhea, respiratory tract infections, dehydration, sprains and fractures, muscular strains, lacerations

✓ High altitude/comprehensive medical kit/ equipment: 41 kinds; oral antibiotics, 8 kinds; injectable medications, 8 kinds; controlled medications, 10 kinds

✓ Logistical support—contracts for commercial air and ground transportation and special equipment

✓ Details of training in Oahu and in Alaska

 UNCLASSIFIED

Conclusion

Team Tibet is prepared to successfully execute the Alaska Training Exercise. Upon conclusion of this exercise, Team Tibet will prepare after action reports and will provide a Mission Confirmation Brief (MCB) to the Commander for his final approval of the Tibet Recovery.

The MCB is tentatively scheduled for 3 August 2004.

Chapter 9

The Hump

Danger in the Air, Boredom on the Ground

*C*BI friends bemoan the lack of interest in our "forgotten" theater. I tell them the CBI is not forgotten, it's "unknown." Talking with visitors at my guest booth in the hangar at the Mid Atlantic Air Museum in Reading, PA every June, I observe that visitors may know a bit about the Flying Tigers. Some may have heard about the Burma Road, General Vinegar Joe Stilwell, Colonel Flip Cochran, Merrill's Marauders, Clair Chennault and the theater's other charismatic leading actors. "But what in the world is the Hump?" they ask.

Photo by Dr. Cordes

Lt. Constein displays CBI/Hump memorabilia at Mid Atlantic Air Museum's WWII Weekend at the Reading (PA) Regional airport. The Cordes lads (L) Connor, 5, and Ryan, 7, asked for his autograph and in turn signed his display board.

ATC Planes Flown on Hump

C-47 (Douglas DC-3)

C-54 (Douglas DC-4)

C-46 (Curtiss Commando)

C-87, C-109 (Both B-24s converted for carrying cargo)

The Air Transport Command flew five models of cargo planes on the Hump; the C-46 became the workhorse, flying mainly out of Chabua, Sookerating, Mohanbari, and Misamari. More C-46s than any other plane crashed or were missing in flight. Some remain unaccounted for. Regardless of which plane they flew, for all Hump pilots and crews the danger was real: flying 500 miles or more over impenetrable jungles, towering mountain peaks, deep ravines, wide, powerful rivers—all in the world's worst flying weather. Contributing to the dangers were inadequate aircraft maintenance so far from the states; underpowered, and in some cases, inadequately tested planes; rudimentary navigation systems; and crowded skies.

Flying on instruments most of the time, the C-46 had frequent icing problems, causing vapor lock in the engines and loss of lift on the wings. At pilot meetings, the crew of 996 probably joined the debates that raged endlessly between those pilots who put on carburetor heat before they entered the weather and those who waited then broke up the ice with the heat. Pilots lucky enough to be flying a plane that had "boots" in working condition could break the ice off the wing by throwing a switch to activate alternating boots.

Unlike today's high-performance jets that can take off even if one engine fails, our propeller-driven planes were underpowered and often overloaded. So takeoff was the crucial moment of the flight. At the end of the runway one day waiting our turn to take off, I witnessed one C-46 struggling on its takeoff run. It just barely lifted off before it reached the end of the runway, flying low and out of sight. In 30 seconds, a huge cloud of black smoke rose ominously a mile or two beyond the runway. It was certain death for the crew, we feared. I learned the next day the copilot was a friend who lived in the same "George Washington Hotel" basha where I was billeted.

In frequent pilot meetings, C-46 pilots were warned of a second danger—aborting a landing in China and "going around" for another attempt. Fields in China were a mile high; at that altitude, our planes had less power than at sea level, especially loaded. If you are too high on the approach, we were instructed, put the plane down anyway, even if you run out of runway! I lost my Chabua chess opponent when, one night at Kunming, he ignored standard procedure and crashed into

71

a Chinese village within the traffic pattern. In flying, as in chess, one wrong move may be fatal.

Our ATC crews consisted of pilot, copilot, radio operator, and, rarely, crew chief or flight engineer. Plane 996 did not have a crew chief on its last flight. Duties of the copilot were to perform operations in flight as directed by the pilot and to read aloud the checklist (and verify procedures orally) before starting engines, before taxiing, during engine run-up, before takeoff, after takeoff, during cruising, before landing, after landing, after shutting down engines, and before leaving the plane.

The radio operator was stationed behind the cockpit bulkhead, just behind the copilot. His job was to control the command radio set used by pilots to talk with the tower. About 10 minutes after takeoff, the radio operator went on his liaison set to call the closest station Army Airways Communication Services for a radio check. Later he'd call in position reports. But unlike present-day FAA airway centers that have all planes on their radar scope and control their speed and direction, AACS did not regulate CBI air traffic. Except for takeoffs and landings controlled by the tower, we were on our own. All our radio operators could do was to monitor air-to-air communications between planes and bases and call Maydays on instructions from the pilot. (It is not known which crewman on 996 called the Mayday.)

In a Mayday or when a crew was lost, the RO held down the liaison transmitter button, permitting three AACS direction-finding teams on the ground to triangulate the signals then inform the RO of the plane's position. (Incidentally, we pilots were never lost; we were just "uncertain of our positions.") After crew chiefs were no longer assigned to flights, some ROs were given additional duties of helping check the plane before takeoff, monitoring fuel supply, and securing the cargo door.

On a rare CFR (contact flight rules) day, even on an IFR (instrument flight rules) day that had little turbulence, flights could become pretty boring for the pilots, the aircraft cruising on autopilot. On most flights, the RO's job was even more boring. Bob Smith from Flatrock, North Carolina, was never bored, never resorted to reading paperbacks. Based at Sookerating, 996's field, he flew 113 trips from December 1943 to September 1944. He may have known the RO *of .996; he may have flown with the pilots a time or two. Using the British crystal-controlled radio aboard the plane, for his own safety and the crew's, Smith took frequent bearings along the route. He became an unofficial navigator.*

We didn't have a navigator in our crews; he would have been of no help whatsoever. Our system of navigation was a blend of dead reckoning and the Bendix Automatic Direction Finder. The ADF worked this way. Along the routes between India and China a number of radio towers were installed, most of them at airfields, shooting a non-directional radio beacon straight up. En route to China and back, pilots tuned their radios to those stations. When the needle of the ADF compass on the instrument panel pointed north, 360 degrees, they were headed directly for the station. When the needle did a 180-degree flip-flop, the pilot knew he was over the station.

The system worked well in clear weather—when you could really do without it! But when the weather was stormy and the sky filled with static electricity, only the Chabua station in India and the Kunming station in China were powerful enough to emit steady, dependable signals. Pilots used dead-reckoning hand-held mechanical D-4 "computers" and acquired a feel for routes, distances, ETAs, winds, position—even when the ADF needle swung wildly. The backup to be used when the needle would not hold steady was to take an "aural null." The pilot reached up to the ceiling over the copilot's seat, tuned to the frequency of the closest radio marker, then slowly rotated a dial until there was no sound whatsoever. The null indicated the direction of the station. I fervently hope all Hump pilots who were lost recalled this seldom-used technique they had learned in training.

CFC: It is gratifying to know that current pilots look at our IFR flying on the Hump as something special. Rick Durden, contributing editor of *IFR, the Magazine for the Accomplished Pilot*, writes in the May, 2003, issue of how we survived with only ADF for navigation. "If pride goeth before the fall," he writes, "it is perhaps wise ...that we pause to give some consideration to what an accomplished pilot is....(The Hump pilot) is a sterling example of members of our fraternity flying regularly in truly awful instrument conditions while dealing with assorted other aeronautical unpleasantness over an extended period of time is now nearly

60 years in our past. As humble seekers of knowledge, it might do us well to tread among those giants of a prior generation and listen to what sort of instrument flying they did, and perhaps learn from it."

Skies over the Hump were crowded, especially from 1944 to the end of the war. Most ATC planes in the CBI skies were flying east-west cargo routes. Cargo planes of other commands, as well as fighters and bombers on tactical missions, often cut across the Hump on their missions to Burma or China. Of course they filed flight plans; the 4th Wing of the Army Airways Communication Service, at least in theory, knew their direction and altitude. But, as I learned, it was prudent to be alert. On one daytime CFR flight to China, halfway across the Hump, the sky filled with broken clouds, a C-47 flew directly in front of us on a southwest course to Burma. We were on autopilot, the pilot taking a nap, I shrieked and. pulled back hard on the control column for all I was worth—one scary near-miss.

A phenomenon that pilots who fly over mountains quickly learn about is updrafts/downdrafts. Certainly the pilots of 996 experienced it at one time or another. My first acquaintance with it came early while I was still working off my copilot requirement. On a rare clear day as we flew to China on autopilot over the high Salween range, I noticed our altitude slowly climbing—without anyone touching the controls and with no change in air speed. I nudged the pilot. He said, "No problem. It's an updraft caused by the west wind striking the cliff. After we cross the peak, we'll come back down." He was right. On the lee side, we dropped gradually to the exact altitude we'd been holding. For a rookie pilot flying west to east, an updraft was a fascinating experience. For a rookie who experienced it for the first time flying east to west, a downdraft was frightening.

In books and in "war stories" at Hump Pilot Association reunions, pilots occasionally refer to downdrafts inside violent storms. My take on that is different. It's certainly true that inside a severe storm Hump planes were tossed up and down like toys, but I think of this action as violent wind shear resulting in turbulence. I believe updrafts/downdrafts to be more likely in clear weather and only when crossing high peaks.

There were nights on the base when I could not escape the grip of fear as I looked to the sky in the east and saw brilliant, terrifying streaks of lightning over the first ridge—and I was scheduled to fly that night! All Hump pilots had their own worries. My biggest was being trapped in a stack of planes waiting to land in low visibility at a base in China. ADF was used for more purposes than simple navigation en route. When you checked in at 18,500 feet approaching Kunming in bad weather, you'd be instructed to descend to, say, 16,000 feet and "hold". You flew out from the beacon for 90 seconds, made a standard-degree turn, returned to the beacon going the opposite direction, flew out again for 90 seconds, turned and continued this racetrack pattern, holding until instructed to descend 500 feet. When all planes beneath you finally landed and you were on the bottom of the stack, you were cleared for landing. But what if a plane above you developed engine trouble and called a Mayday? Now was the time to worry. Cleared to land, the plane in trouble would descend pell-mell through the stack—on instruments!

Dangers led inevitably to fatal crashes and bailouts. Statistics are not firm, but more than 500 planes crashed or were reported missing in cargo missions on the Hump and on bomber and fighter missions against enemy targets in the CBI. More than 1,300 crewmen were killed in crashes or failed to return from flights or bailouts. Another 1,100 walked out after bailing out. About 400 are still missing. Aircraft 996 was one of 35 Sookerating C-46s included in that record, according to The Aluminum Trail *by Chick Marrs Quinn. Quinn, whose husband, 1st Lt Loyal Stuart Marrs, Jr,. was pilot of C-109 tanker 2000, a B-24 modified to transport gasoline, that crashed en route from Jorhat, India, to Chanyi, China, on February 27, 1945. It was Marr's 56th Hump trip.*

In her book, Quinn talks about the next-to-last flight of #2000. Over Fort Hertz, Burma, the radio operator spotted gasoline spraying off the trailing edge of the wing. The pilot, Lt Richard Kurzenberger, made an immediate 180 and returned to Jorhat. After the plane landed, the expediting officer entered the cockpit, ran up the engines, and declared the plane fit for flight. Kurzenberger and his crew were ordered to report to the C.O. the following morning and another crew was called to take the flight. Lt. Marrs was the pilot. Kurzenberger and his crew watched in apprehension and silence as 2000 took off at about 11pm. It was to be the plane's last flight.

Quinn went beyond searching for details of her young husband's crash. She spent nearly 10 years painstakingly searching through more than 60,000 pages of government documents for details of other crashes and planes missing in flight. Few accident loss reports were filed before June 1943, she cautions, and not all crashes or planes missing in action were reported.

For each event, she states the date, type and tail number of the plane (transports, bombers, fighters, and a few miscellaneous), the takeoff and destination fields, the place of the accident, and names and serial numbers of crewmembers. Many relatives of victims have been in touch with Quinn, some visiting her to thank her in person.

CFC: *The Aluminum Trail,* the title of Quinn's book, was a phrase used in the CBI to describe the trail of wreckage of crashed planes visible from the air. Not all C-46s were finished in airliner aluminum; at least half, I judge, were olive drab camouflage, making spotting impossible among the variegated cliffs and peaks of the mighty Himalayas. On my 96 round-trip flights I never once saw a crashed plane on the Hump, aluminum or camouflage!

The first C-46 event reported in Quinn's book is the bailout of 17 passengers and three crewmen of C-46 #2420 en route from Chabua, India, my home base, to Kunming, China, on 2 August 1943. Among the passengers were American military personnel, two high-ranking Chinese army officers, two American diplomats, one the chief political aide to Chiang Kai Shek, and Eric Severeid, war correspondent who later became a well-known TV journalist. When the plane lost its left engine, the pilot attempted to return to Chabua but lost too much altitude to continue. All passengers and crew except the copilot bailed out into Burma; the copilot was killed in the crash. An Army Air Corps surgeon and two medics parachuted in to tend to the injured radio operator. In two weeks a Search and Rescue party reached the group, and after 10 days and 140 miles of walking on rough trails, the group reached safety.

CFC: In his WWII memoir *Not So Wild a Dream,* Severeid includes a 50-page detailed, brilliant, at times lyrical, chapter about that adventure of a lifetime, as only a first-rate writer can. It is far and away the most descriptive narrative I've read about what it's like to bail out over the

Hump—landing perilously close to enemy-held territory, organizing the bailouts for survival, living for a couple weeks with Naga tribesmen feared to be headhunters, and finally trudging to safety.

The flight began easily enough. "We took off smoothly and rose into a downy lather of mist and delicate streamers of white cloud." Severeid wondered whether any of the peaks to the north were Everest. (Of course none was; Everest is 500 miles west of our bases in Assam.) An hour later, the left engine went out, the pilot ordered all baggage overboard, and a mass bailout followed. Except for the near-miracle of a clear, sunny day in the midst of the monsoon season, the saga might have ended differently, for within an hour, a C-47 overhead dropped a streamer with a note instructing the group how to signal with parachute panels, and promising rescue.

The C-47 returned for a second drop: two bales attached to bright orange chutes—a radio receiver, a Gibson Girl transmitter (which unfortunately broke on contact), two Springfield rifles, and a third bale with legs—Col Don Flickinger, wing flight surgeon!

Severeid goes beyond exposition to reveal his feelings and fears. He became lead organizer, chaplain, recorder, negotiator with the Naga tribesmen about working for pay, and took his turn on guard duty. The author was not shy in expressing himself about social problems he observed in the CBI nor about military inefficiencies. When he discovered the jungle kit in the backpack of his chute was empty, the machete, rations, first-aid kit and other vital essentials missing, he bemoaned the state of discipline at the Chabua air base. I experienced my own frustrations in my year there.

Quinn's book includes reports on hundreds of fatal crashes and missing planes. Most were ATC cargo planes based on the India side of the Hump—C-47s, C-46s, C-87s, C-109s, and C-54s. There are, in addition, numerous reports on losses of bombers and fighters— B-24s, B-25s, B-29s, P-38s, P-51s, P-40s, P-47s, P-61s, A-26s, as well as several liaison L-1s and L-5s, and trainers PT-17s, PT-19s, AT-6s.

From the start of the Hump in 1942 through 1945, Sookerating lost 35 of its C-46s. (Chabua, next door where I was stationed, lost 33.) Twenty of Sookerating's airplane losses came before the doomed flight of 996 on November 3, 1944. Twenty of Sookerating's 35 were crashes, six were bailouts/crashes, one was a collision with a C-109, and eight are missing.

The always-present fantasy of every Hump pilot was to get to that magic number of flight hours that would send him home--750. In 1942 and 1943 the number was fewer. I recall my month living in a British presidio outside Karachi awaiting assignment to the Hump. There we met a dozen pilots on their way stateside after only six months and 550 hours on the Hump. The requirements increased gradually—600, 650, 700, and finally, my requirement, 750 hours. Commanding General Tunner added one more nice little wrinkle— remain at the base for one year!

My magic moment came at exactly 4 p.m. on July 28, 1945, while I was halfway across the Hump coming back from Kunming. I savored the moment and still recall it clearly. But for three months after that, I was forced into a belittling, no-account assignment. Spotting a degree in education in my personnel file, the base commander made me assistant training officer. It might have been fun, but there wasn't a single airman to be trained! The training officer and I sat in our little office five days a week, 8 to 5, without a phone, without files, doing absolutely nothing. The right way and the Army way. We flew four hours a month to qualify for flight pay, heading west in the valley on low-priority flights.

On the Ground

I still find it hard to believe I never flew into another ATC base in eastern India, not even into Sookerating next door, the base of 996. Not only were we isolated from other bases, we were isolated from the world—nothing like the harsh isolation of the men of Team Tibet during their mission, true, but they at least had news sent to them electronically. Without radios and newspapers, the war in Europe and the Pacific was not on our scopes, although really big news, like the surrender of Japan, drifted to us in a day or two. Letters from home, precious letters, were really our only contact with the outside world. Mail call was the highlight of every day.

CFC: I recently discovered a 60-year-old note in my pocket logbook that reveals, with a touch of wit, the preciousness of daily mail call. I was apparently free to go to mail call on a day four basha-mates were not. The note to the mail sergeant, signed by J.S. Bird, W.N.

Hanahan, J. Fattaleh, and Preston, read, "Give him our mail, DAMN IT."

Life between flights was boring. "Boring" was good compared to conditions our fighting troops endured, and we knew it. We were thankful we had our own beds to sleep in.

The crewmen of 996 were stationed at Sookerating, AF Base Unit 1337. Like Chabua, the single runway, the barracks, the flight line buildings—all were carved out of a plantation of Assam tea, prized the world over. Areas not used by the AAC remained planted in tea. At harvest time, young mothers, their babies strapped on their backs, cackled ceaselessly as they plucked the tender tea leaves.

Photo by George Wenrich
Like many ATC fields in India, Sookerating AAF Base Unit 1337 was carved out of a British plantation. Pilots lived in Old Tent City or New Tent City until they had enough seniority to move into a tea plantation building like this one.

The pilots of 996 were probably quartered in British double-layer tents with concrete floors in Old Tent City or New Tent City. Or they might have been housed in a four-man "basha" hut, (bamboo, thatched-roof, built without nails). If they were lucky, they stayed in the British tea planter's family bungalow, actually a large house accommodating 35 pilots, or in what had once been a tea plantation carriage house. They slept without sheets on a low wooden bed called a charboy, with a mosquito "bar" tucked in on all sides, and latticed ropes for a mattress.

79

Photo by Roger Johnson
Soookerating Airfield, looking south. 1ˢᵗ Troop Carrier was located on the south side. ATC Headquarters was just south of the flight line.

The crew of 996 were probably not as lucky as Bud Speidel, a C-47 Hump pilot- friend of mine who, with three other officers, lived off base in a tea plantation cottage. Befriended by the English manager of the plantation and his wife, they were frequently invited to the "big house" for tea and dinner.

The 996 crew ate in one of several small mess halls. As we did at Chabua, they probably contributed a few rupees a month so the mess sergeant could supplement the Quartermaster food (a lot of Spam) with eggs, onions, cucumbers, maybe even an occasional chicken. At every meal they found on the mess-hall tables bottles of Atabrine to ward off malaria from the ubiquitous mosquitoes. Most of us who eventually made it home attracted stares wherever we went because of our strange, medicinally--induced yellow skins. From time to time, the 996 crew may have taken the shuttle to the "One Wing Low" Chinese restaurant just off the runway. When transportation was available, they may also have gone to a Chinese restaurant in Dibrugargh, by Indian standards a fair-size town.

CFC: Information conditions at Sookerating were graciously provided to me by two C-46 pilots who were stationed there: Jay Vinyard, current president of the CBI Hump Pilots Association, Amarillo, Texas, and George Wenrich, long-time friend from Ashburn, Virginia,

Photo by George Wenrich
**Dibragargh. Dirt, merchants, villagers, and sacred cows (not shown here)
blend together in a picturesque, if odoriferous, melee.**

*Life on the base was dull, dreary—and hot and wet in the
summer. Afternoon temperatures were over 100 degrees; the
monsoon wind brought in 100 inches of rain in both July and August.
Most men went to the movies whenever they could—except in the
summer when they couldn't take the heat inside the building.*

*The pilots led lonely lives on the ground, choosing their own
way to pass the time—reading, a little bridge, maybe chess. Many
played poker, especially on payday. A section of the new bamboo
building near the main mess hall was set off as an Officers Club,
with a bar, but there wasn't much liquor to drink. There was no "top
shelf."*

*The closest town, a half hour's hike from the base, was a dirty
little bamboo village with a fascinating name—"Doom Dooma." The
996 fellows might have gone there from time to time out of sheer
boredom on the base or because they simply couldn't take being
cooped up in a tiny, windowless tent or basha hut. In the heart of
Doom Dooma was a bazaar with dirty merchants, their lips stained by
betel nuts, selling an array of silver jewelry and bangles, condiments,
and other products. Stench from the condiments, the charcoal
burning in braziers, the droppings of sacred cows who were free to
roam wherever they chose—all made nasal navigation to the town a
reality.*

If they'd had enough time in the CBI to qualify, the crewmen of 996 may have caught a break: they may have gone on rest leave to Shillong in the Khasi Hills, or, even more beautiful, to Darjeeling, near the Tibetan border. If it was Darjeeling, they had an unforgettable toy-line train ride up the mountain before checking in at the Mount Everest Hotel. If the cloud curtain ever parted, they might have gotten an awesome glimpse of Kinchinjunga, the most massive of the Himalayan peaks, the third highest mountain in the world.

If they went on leave to Shillong, they may have had as liberating, as wonderful, a break as I had in June of 1945. High in the mountains, Shillong is the summer capital of India, a mile above sea level, an enclave of Indian Christians. The 996 crew would have stayed in the charming Fernwood Hotel, owned and graciously managed by a Swiss couple. Thanks to the generosity of a maharajah who made his estate available to the Allied military, I played tennis every day on eight beautiful clay courts, a few rounds of golf, bridge in the "whist" room of the maharajah's clubhouse, and enjoyed a Saturday night dance in the clubhouse ballroom. Best of all were the scrumptious dinners served in the hotel by turbaned Punjabis, preceded by cocktails and gracious sociability with British military officers and civil servants. At the end of the leave, we dragged ourselves back to our bases, our B-4 bags full of memories to cherish. The objective now was to get to that magic number of 750 flight hours and go home.

Loneliness was especially cruel in the still-dark early mornings when the CQ shined his flashlight on our faces. "Lieutenant, your turn to fly." Preferring light clothes for flying to the bulky, thick fleece-lined winter outfits, you put on your khaki shirt and pants, squeezed into your flight suit and leather jacket, and slung your .45 automatic holster over a shoulder. Streaks of lightning emphasized your black mood. You reached for your bag and threw in your parachute, oxygen mask, and now that fleece-lined flight pants and jacket you'd be glad to have if you had to bail out. At 20,000 feet the temperature is under zero. Thank goodness for the efficient cockpit heater. The sergeant jeeped you to Operations on the flight line.

Photo Courtesy of George Wenrich

George Wenrich on his way to the flight line at Sookerating. The barracks bag slung over his shoulder contained, among other items, a winter fleece-lined flight suit—information of consequence to Captain Kent and Dr. Tyrell at the crash site.

In spite of our sparse living conditions—the 996 crew at "Sook", me at Chabua—it was our home away from home. Like the rest of us, Rich Nethaway, a C-46 pilot also stationed at Chabua, wrote me about his Hump experience, including a bailout over China on his 22nd mission. (See pages 139-144 of my Tales of the Himalayas.*) He ends the letter with a tribute to his brother-in-law, who was in on the Normandy landings. I agree completely with his sentiments.*

"Let me acknowledge that if I had to do it all over again, I would change nothing. Would I exchange my assignment for a trek across North Africa and on up through Italy? I don't think so.

"Consider life and danger on an aircraft carrier—an airplane mechanic, a cook, or any of several thousand sailors deep in the bowels of the ship. The ship comes under air attack. The decks above are afire, explosions set off minute by minute. Or suppose you are in a submarine. Destroyers above you dump depth charges.

"Or suppose you are in a landing craft heading toward a heavily fortified Pacific beach or Normandy.

"Or you're in a bomber over Germany. A fighter has knocked out your plane and you bail out. Picture the terror of being a prisoner of war or, even worse, subjected to a death march.

83

"I stand in absolute awe of these men. We had barracks and beds to sleep in every night, hot meals, showers, clean sheets, movies, candy, beer, and sunshine. Many of them had snow or intense heat, mud, dirty clothes, C- rations, and lonely weeks and months in foxholes under heavy, relentless shelling or mortar fire.

"I thank God for my job on the Himalayan Hump."

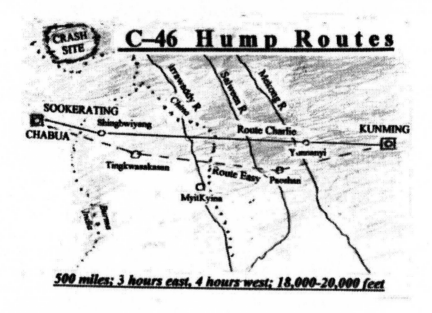

Chapter 10

Mountain Training in Alaska

In June, Team Tibet 2004 team deployed to Alaska for 19 days of mountain training at Black Rapids Training Center (BRTC) and Denali National Park. Instruction was provided by the Northern Warfare Training Center based in Fort Wainright, Fairbanks. A few months earlier, Captain Kent had received an e-mail and four attachments from SFC Steven Decker of NWTC outlining the schedule, individual gear required, operations order for the trip on Kahitna Cilhi glacier, and the training plan.

Photo from Army News Service
Team Tibet 2004 heads toward Mount McKinley for mountain training.

The training plan was drawn up by SFC Decker and two civilian mountaineers on the NWTC staff, Pete Smith and Mark Gilbertson. As early as a year before they presented the plan, they discussed with Capt Kent and his staff the need for rigorous physical training by the team in Hawaii before they arrived in Alaska. At the start of the training, the NWTC trainers—SSG Beemster was the fourth—were impressed with the team's condition. Gilbertson said, "We pretty much tortured them on the mountain. I guess they busted their butts in PT in Hawaii, because they showed up really well in Alaska."

The schedule called for the team to arrive in Fairbanks on Thursday, 10 June. Training began the following day.

11 June:	0900-1100	Last minute purchase of equipment
	1300-1300	Deploy to Black Rapids Training Center/ Lunch en route
	1400-1400	Issue equipment
	1500-1500	Risk management
	1600-1600	Mountain medical
	1730-1730	Rope management and knots
	1830-1830	Supper
	1830-UTC	Hike to Pole 16 (UTC: Until complete)
12 June	0800-1100	Climbing at rock site
	1100-1200	Lunch
	1200-1300	Move on fixed rope
	1330-1500	Rappels
	1500-1630	Package a casualty
	1630-1800	Move to triathlon site
	1800-UTC	Set up camp/supper
13 June	0800-1100	Triathlon
	1200-1200	Move to BRTS
	1300-1300	Lunch
	1500-1500	River crossing
	1500-UTC	Recovery
14 June	0800-UTC	Move to WF 635290; begin movement of route flamer
15 June	0800-UTC	Move on route flamer

16 June	0800-UTC	Move on route flamer
17 June	0800-0900	Redeploy FDA
	0900-UTC	Recover
18 June	0900-1100	Draw MAT gear
	1100-UTC	Prep for Kahiltna
19 June	0900-1030	Fly to Talkeetna
	1200-1200	National Park Service orientation
	1330-1330	Lunch
	1400-1400	Fly to Kahiltna Glacier
	1600-1600	Establish base camp (6800 feet)
	1700-1700	Crevasse rescue
	1830-1830	Glacier movement in area
	1830-UTC	AAR, retraining, supper
20 June	0700-0900	Wake-up, breakfast
	0900-UTC	Establish base camp 1 (7800 feet)
21 June	0700-0900	Wake-up, breakfast
	0900-UTC	Carry to camp 2, cache, return camp
22 June	0700-0900	Wake-up, breakfast
	0900-UTC	Move to camp 2 (9800 feet)
23 June	0700-0900	Wake-up, breakfast
	0900-UTC	Move to camp 3 (11,000 feet)
24 June	Rest Day	
25 June	0700-0900	Wake-up, breakfast
	0900-UTC	Move to camp 4 and return
26 June	0700-0900	Wake-up, breakfast
	0900-UTC	Return to base camp
27 June	0700-0900	Wake-up, breakfast
	0900-1300	Prep for fly-out
	1430-1430	Return FWA
	1830-1830	Recovery
	1830-UTC	Prep for actual mission

Operations order for training on the Kahiltna glacier was spelled out in five sections

1. Situation

Enemy Forces: None

Terrain: Steep mountainous terrain with deep snow cover and heavily glaciated

Weather: Day temperatures are in the 40-50 degree range with night temperatures in the single digits. Above 10,000 feet temperatures can frequently drop below 0 at night and rise to the 30s as the sun comes up. The constant snow cover will enhance the sunlight, making temperatures feel much hotter in the daylight, causing sunburn. Wind can be particularly fast in the vicinity of Windy Corner (13,000 feet).

Purpose: The expedition will deploy via CH-47 (Helicopter) and by foot to the 14,000-foot Basin Camp on Kahiltna glacier in order to expose members to the effects of high altitude environment. A summit attempt of Denali is not the purpose of this training event.

2. Mission

NWTC will conduct a high altitude foot movement on Flamingo via NV 895810 to NV 975945 19-26 June in order to expose the members of the recovery team to the effects of high altitude, validate members of the team and the unit's train-up plan.

3. Execution

Commander's intent: The expedition will move up the Kahiltna glacier on foot to the 14,000-foot camp, carrying their equipment and establishing camps along the route.

Concept of Operation

Phase 1: Planning

Phase 1 will commence with the coordination for food, fuel, national Park Service permits, and accommodations. NWTC coordinates.
Phase 2: Movement
Movement will commence at 0900 hours 19 June at Bldg. 3749 FWA. Personal gear will be loaded, and upon completion, departure will be initiated. CH-47 will fly to Talkeetna for fuel. The expedition will attend the briefing at the National Park Service. A weather call will be made by the pilots. Upon notification of suitable weather, insertion on the Kahiltna Glacier south of the park will be made, and the expedition will move IAW the training schedule. NWTC will provide five mountaineers as rope team leaders, hardware for team members, and guidance to JPAC for equipment. JPAC will submit to NWTC by 1 Mar 04 a National Park Service permit form for each member. NPS will allow one change-out of personnel up to 30 days out. Team members should read the NPS booklet at: http: www.nps.gov/den/home/mountaineering/booklet.mbenglish.html

CFC: The booklet is a comprehensive National Park Service guide to climbing Mt. McKinley, at 20,320 feet North America's highest peak. The native American word for the mountain is Denali, the "High One." From May through July, a thousand mountaineers take to the big hill, climbing routes West Buttress, West Rib, Cassin, or Muldrow.

As a pilot who flew at high altitudes over the Himalayas, I was interested in the explanation of the effect latitude has on barometric pressure. Denali is located at latitude 63 N, Mt. Everest 27 N. The closer one gets to the equator, the lower the barometric pressure for a given altitude. Thus, according to Dr. Peter H. Hackett writing in the NPS guide, Denali's 20,320-foot summit would be 21,000–23,000 feet in the Himalayas. Since lower barometric pressure yields less oxygen in the air, he asserts that a climber at Denali would have less oxygen than a climber would have at the same altitude in the Himalayas. Dr. Hackett alludes to the health factor of hypoxemia.

4. Service Support

Concept of support: FIX: As necessary, utilizing organic   unit assets. FUEL: All military/GSA vehicles utilized will top off tanks as necessary. All white gas will be carried by the expedition members. FEED: The expedition will carry all food required for the duration of the mission.

Materials and Services

Class I: Each expedition member will receive a mixture of MCWs (Meals, Cold Weather) and A-rations from Sgt Thatcher

Class III: Coleman fuel will be procured at BRTS.

Class V: None

Class VI: Deploy with sufficient hygiene items

Class VIII: Immediate first-aid requirements will be met on site by qualified personnel.

Medical Evacuation

Evacuation Priority: Ground via sled to NPR ranger station at 7,200 feet or 14,000 feet, then, if necessary, by air coordinated through NPS. Procedures: Stabilize with Wilderness First Responders, initiate a ground evacuation utilizing available team members. If medevac is required, NPS will make all necessary co-ordinations and relay information to the expedition

Transportation:

Transportation to and from Route Flamingo via CH-47 from 4-123 AVN. Ground transportation will be via GSA vehicle from NWTC.

5. Command and Signal

Command: Peter Smith, Mark Gilbertson then by rank among the rope leaders.

Signal: All communications with FWA will be via satellite telephone (primary). Satellite instructions are attached to this Operations Order. Alternate communications can be obtained from NPS but only in an extreme emergency.

STEVEN DECKER
SFC, USA
ALASKA MT TR
NCOIC

A: JTFFA required clothing
B: NWTC provided equipment
C: Training schedule

ANNEX A. This should be the same gear intended for use in Tibet as outlined in the Sleeping Gear list.
Polypropylene top and bottom
Goretex top and bottom
Gloves
Balaclava
8 pr wool or polypropylene socks
2 one-quart nalgene bottles with covers
Hygiene items
Seat harness
Fleece top
Fleece bottom
Tents
Stoves
Fuel bottles
Cook sets

ANNEX B
Avalanche beacons and probes
Snow shovels
Snow saws

Altimeters
Mittens with liners
GPS
Satellite telephone with instruction sheet
Mt. McKinley A-3, Talkeetna D-3 map sheets
VS-17
Overshoes
Snow pickets
Ropes
Carabiners
Webbing
Snowshoes
Sleds
Plastic mountaineering boots
Crampons
Ice axes
Sleeping bag rated to at least –20 degrees

Individual Gear List

Each member of the Tibet team should have the following gear. Brand names for clothing are not set in stone; they are guidelines based on experience.

Sleeping gear

1 Mountain Hardware, 3rd Dimension Zero, or Northface Snowshoe
1 OR basic Bivy, Mountain Hardware, or Conduit SL Bivy
1 Thermarest Ridgerest or Z Rest

Packs and Accessories

1 Dana design Astralplane
2 OR water bottle pockets
1 OR Hydroseal pack cover L
2 OR Hydorseal compression stiff sack #3
1 Camelback Classic
1 Headlamp, any kind, with replacements bulbs

Clothing

Boots **must** be fitted and broken in prior to mission. Sturdy rough trail hikers with waterproof uppers. Check the Backpacker Magazine 2004 gear guide for choices—Lowa, La Sportiva, Merrel, Scarpa

1 Polypro beanie hat OR, Mountain Headware, North Face
10 Smartwool, Wigwam, or Thorlo backpacker socks
1 OR Crocodile gaiters
2 OR Windstopper gloves
1 Mountain Hardware Chugach or military polartec fleece
12 Mid-weight long underwear, OR Mountain Hardware, Patagonia
1 Camp booties or sneakers
Harness—of the Alpine variety, fitted to each person
No sport climbing. Black Diamond
Bod or Alpine Bod
1 pearabiner
50 six mil cordalette per person

Group Gear

Cooking:
7 MSR Whisperlite International with repair kit
7 MSR fuel bottle, 22 oz.
7 MSR Alpine cookset
14 thirty-two-once Nalgene bottles

Rock Gear
2 each size Black Diamond pitons: Lost Arrow, Angle, Bugaboo
Knifeblade
2 set Black Wired Stopper
2 spool 9/16 webbing

2 spool 1" webbing
50 aluminum oval carabiners
4 one hundred-sixty-five inch 10 mil rope
2 rock hammers
2 rock hand drills
30 rock bolts

Tent

2 Black Diamond Megamid (for cooking in weather)
7 Mountain Hardware Trango 3.1 or North Face VE-25
7 Footprint for tent
1 Mountain Hardware Spacestation (for group meetings)

Miscellaneous

100 Sealine Boundry 115 dry bags for carrying expedition equipment. Can be used for man pack or mules
2 Dry bag repair kit
5 Camelback bite valve
2 Tent repair kit

Chapter 11

Mountaineers/Linguist

Mark Gilbertson is a civilian mountaineer who works for the Northern Warfare Training Center in Alaska. As instructors for Team Tibet in Alaska, he and SSG Beemster got to know the team well even before they deployed to Tibet with them.

Mark enlisted in the Army MPs in 1995, serving at multiple bases in multiple deployments. He ended up reenlisting in 2000 for Fort Wainright, Fairbanks, Alaska. For Mark, it turned out to be the right place at the right time, for the NWTC was just then coming up to Alaska and needed a non-commissioned-officer-in-charge.

Want to be a mountaineering and cold-weather instructor? he was asked. Mark jumped at the chance and served in the assignment for three years. Even though normally the position is an infantry slot, his MOS of MP was not a deterrent. While he was the only instructor with an MP beside his name, there were other instructors with MOSs unrelated to mountain warfare training. He said drolly, "I spent four years not being an MP."

But his MP classification had a drastic effect later. When he was about to leave the service, the Iraq business started up, and the Army imposed a stop-loss order. A year was added to Mark's contract;

he was sent to Fort Polk, Louisiana, then to Baghdad. He did a tour, came back, the stop-loss order was lifted, and he left the service.

While he was on terminal leave, remarkably, a position opened for mountaineering instructor back in Alaska. Wow! he thought. He applied immediately and has been back in his old job in NWTC, this time as a civilian. He'd been gone only eight months. Totally, for four years he's been training soldiers to climb, ski, snow-shoe, and maneuver in cold weather. For soldiers who never operated in cold weather, he's taught them to prepare food and shelter, to take care of injuries, to build fighting positions.

A problem that goes with training in Alaska is that scaling Mt. McKinley is so appealing some commanders think of it as adventure training and will not sign off on it. That was not the case for the training of Team Tibet 2004, Mark added.

The concept of mountain warfare training, Mark explained, came from WWII experiences. A school was opened in Alaska in 1948, the active-duty Army's only school of the kind. The National Guard has one in Vermont, and the Marine corps has its in California.

In 2002 Mark was on a mission to recover nine Navy personnel in Laos. That experience and his varied service in the military, he believes, have helped him greatly in getting along well with soldiers without causing any tension between civilians and the military.

Mountaineer Gilbertson was the only member of the 2002 Rouse team to serve on the squad that investigated the site Team Tibet 2004 will excavate. The Chinese who took them to the site had done their homework, obviously having gone there several times, Mark said. The contingent consisted of an Army major, a couple other Chinese, and a group of Tibetans. It rained constantly for the first three days. Yet the captain went to the site in nearly zero visibility. It was near the beginning of October, just starting to get cold and to snow. On the way out the weather was clear, so Mark has the route pretty well memorized.

This 2004 site is much more dangerous than the 2002 site, Mark said, even though the 2002 site is 1500 feet higher. The site to be excavated is much less accessible and more difficult to reach because it's four days back in the mountain. There will be no medevac, no air support. On the second day's hike in 2002, the investigative team had to negotiate a 6-inch ledge that runs more than 100 feet. He and Sgt Beemster plan to leave early on the second day of the 2004 mission to set pitch lines with intermediate anchors so everyone has a line to hang on to.

At both the first site and the new site there had been scavenging, not as much at the second because it was be too difficult to carry anything heavy from this remote site. The party found sheaths, but all knives and guns carried by crewmen were missing, as were fabrics and parachutes. That was understandable, for China had not yet annexed Tibet in the 1940s, and it was difficult to obtain fabrics in remote places. Mark was surprised to see that tires were still there, although the inner tube from the tail section tire was missing.

Mark was born in 1975 at the Lamoore Naval Air Station in California, where his father served. The Navy brat left California at age 5. He has lived in Japan, New York, Maryland, and places in between. His dad retired to Maryland; Mark graduated from high school there. He attended the University of West Virginia as music major, the violin his performance instrument. He has an extensive music collection, mostly classical. Of course he has an abiding interest in mountaineering, summer and winter, as well as in snow-shoeing, skiing, and ice-climbing. He is also a gun collector and target-shooter.

In his sometime duty in Hawaii, he enjoys days in paradise. "But I'd rather be in Alaska," he said.

∧∧∧

Like his fellow mountaineer Mark Gilbertson, Army Staff Sergeant **Gary Beemster** likes living in Alaska. So does his family. He enjoys taking his wife, Janet, and their two-year-old son and four-year-old daughter trotting through the mountains. "Janet is starting to get into it now," he said. "I like showing them what I do for a living. And it's all free entertainment!"

Gary's Army service was not his first stint living in Alaska. He was born in 1973 in Spokane, Washington, and pretty much grew up in the area. His father serving in the Air Force, the family moved to Anchorage then back to Idaho, 200 or so miles from Spokane.

Gary joined the Army in 1991 and was a ground-pounder for 11 years. He served in the Berlin Brigade and then moved around in Fort Campbell, Kentucky, with 11 Bravo Infantry. He has been to Korea and to a couple places the military deemed it was necessary for him to go—the Cobart Towers bombing in Saudi Arabia and some "skirmishes here and there."

His luck changed in 2002. Stationed at Fort Wainright, Alaska, as Platoon Sergeant with the 101st Infantry, he met a couple guys who worked at the Northern Warfare Training Center there. Sgt Cruz, who had been on the 2002 mission to Tibet, was the first buddy to rave about his mountaineer assignment. Gary figured it was time to do something a little different, so he pursued an assignment with NWTC. They signed him on, and he's been happy about it ever since.

Even before becoming an active mountaineer instructor, Gary was into physical fitness and earned an associate degree in fitness in a military school. Since then he's earned college credits through "E Army U," an online program that allows soldiers to access courses at about 50 colleges. Taking courses at night and whenever he can, he is now just 13 credits short of completing his bachelor's degree, majoring in history.

The Tibet 2004 mission will be Gary's first. He and Mountaineer Gilbertson will help smooth the way for the team to negotiate the tough spots and to cross rivers en route to the crash site. Once there, they will join the team, as every member will, in the nearly sacred work of searching for remains and artifacts.

Being chosen out of all the instructors NWTC has on its staff was a lucky break, he said. He was happy too that on his first mission he will be side-by-side with experienced mission veterans, including the photographer and mortuary affairs specialist who made the 2002 Tibet mission.

"To have an opportunity to do this, to travel to China—it's a dream come true," he said, "and will save me thousands of travel dollars in addition. In a heartbeat, any of us here would have jumped at this chance, this honor."

Gary bought a digital camera for this once-in-a-lifetime crack at the awesome beauty of the Himalayas. The photographs will be the main attraction in his extensive collection. When he returns, he will immediately pick up on other hobbies—rock climbing, playing soccer, chalk drawing, and the "biggest hobby of all—my family."

∧∧∧

Linguist on Team Tibet is **Cpl Ng Yu Ling.** Twenty-one-year-old Ng, who was born in Canton, China, lists Brooklyn, NY, as his hometown. His family consists of his mother, father, and brother.

Ng had a year of college before joining the Marines on June 24, 2002. After finishing boot camp at Parris Island, South Carolina, in September, he was assigned Marine Combat Training in North Carolina. After MOS school, in January 2003 he was sent to his first duty station, Camp Kinser, Okinawa, where he underwent field training, including combat skill, navigation, and much more.

JPAC in Hawaii has on board linguists for most countries in which it conducts MIA missions, but none for China. Ng was surprised to get a phone call in Okinawa telling him he was picked to join the team, one of five augmentees. In addition to English, he speaks Mandarin; he received no special training for the mission. As the lowest rank on the mission, and the youngest, he expects to learn a great deal from the other members, and to get outstanding training and experience he could get no other way. He looks forward eagerly to the mission and considers it an honor to serve.

(After the expedition, Geoff Kent told me how important Ng was on the mission. "Even though he spoke only Mandarin," Geoff said, "we had no problems in translation between ourselves, the Chinese team, and Tibetans. If Tibetan laborers did not understand Mandarin, Ng found someone who did and the two engaged in double translation. We could not have done without him.")

Ng said he is interested in almost everything. He enjoys sports, especially handball, basketball, and volleyball, and he is an ardent chess player.

Connections

Mark Gilbertson: *(1) A military connection between us is that we were both MPs. I guarded coal piles at the Philadelphia Electric Company for a few months, he served in Iraq and elsewhere. (2) But our civilian occupations could not be further apart. He spends time working in the high, cold mountains; I spent years as a teacher, then more years as a school superintendent, which, in the Sizzling Sixties, was anything but a cold job. (3) A bond between us is our love of classical music, mine beginning in junior high, 41 years before he was born.. We both like Haydn. He prefers the string quartets, I the piano sonatas.*

Gary Beemster: *(1) Gary and I share love of family as our most precious gift. (2) We agree on pursuing education, and we both like travel.*

Ng Yu Ling: *Ng has an interest in chess, one of the world's oldest and most popular board games worldwide. In foreign travel after the war, I observed chess in public parks everywhere. I don't play any longer, but whenever the word is mentioned I think of my ATC chess buddy in India. He was killed in a landing accident in Kunming China.*

Chapter 12

The Hump

World's Worst Flying Weather

*Graduation is a happy, exciting occasion, no less in Aviation
Cadet training in WWII than in high school or college
today. If the pilots of 996 were Aviation Cadet graduates, they would
have nervously paced the assembly hall of their Advanced Training
base after the graduation ceremony, eagerly waiting to have their
wings and gold second lieutenant's bars pinned on their spanking new
uniforms. And they awaited one more thing—their orders. Single-
engine graduates looked forward to being top gun fighter pilots. An
unlucky few would draw the dreaded assignment of instructor pilot.
Multi-engine graduates knew they'd become bomber pilots, instructor
pilots, target-tow pilots, cargo pilots, or ferry pilots.*

*Graduating airmen were aware of the bases to which they
might be sent for transition training. The base multi-engine pilots
didn't want to see on their orders was Reno, Nevada. But for the
pilots of 996, if they had indeed been Cadets, that was their first
station. Like all of us, they knew that meant being sent to India to fly
the daunting and legendary Hump. At least their orders for a delay en
route would give them a week or so at home first.*

*Reno was chosen as a base for C-46 training base because
the Sierra Nevada Mountains could simulate, if modestly, the mighty
Himalayas where its pilots were headed. Coming from the small twin-
engine AT-11s or AT-17s in Advanced Training, all of us were in awe*

of the behemoth Curtiss Commando—108-foot wingspan, cockpit 20 feet off the ground, two huge 2,000 HP engines. After a mere six weeks in Reno, we left for Karachi, India, our ultimate destination probably Sookerating, Chabua, Mohanbari, or Misamari.

En route to Karachi, a Douglas four-engine C-54 carried us comfortably on the Crescent Run from Miami. We stayed over in the exotic cities of Casablanca, Tripoli, Cairo, Abadan. In Karachi I was assigned to Chabua. The home base of 996 was Sookerating, a few miles northeast of Chabua. Both bases were developed on lush tea plantations. Checkout as first pilot on the C-46 would come months later after 200 hours of scary on-the-job-flight training over the Himalayas. Meanwhile, we'd fly the right seat as copilots.

If the 1337th AAFBU at Sookerating was like my 1333rd AAFBU at Chabua, the pilots of Sook 996 got a less-than-welcome reception on their arrival. I hope they weren't given as tough a time as I was—I had to scrounge around to find my own bunk! It was late October 1944.

A few days later I was scheduled to make my first flight. The date was November 3—the date of 996's last flight! I remember well the stormy weather that night as we took off.

In Operations just before 1900 hours, I met the pilot as he filed a flight plan. It was raining, hard. The weather was foul, scary; streaks of lightning split the night sky, followed by peals of thunder booming like tribal drums. We left Operations and a jeep carried us to the flight line. Hail pelted the canvas top, sheets of rain blew in through the cracks. Cleared for takeoff, Capt Owens shoved the throttles hard. A crosswind tugged on the big bird as she lumbered down the runway. Heavily loaded with twenty-two 55-gallon drums of gasoline, we reached 85 mph and lifted off. Within minutes we were in pea soup, on instruments. As we climbed, we were tossed about like a toy—a deluge of water, a howling snowstorm, ice driving against the windshield and already forming on the wings. At 6,000 feet the airspeed dropped to near stalling at 80 mph then rushed past a redlined 280 mph. We rose and dove like a roller coaster. When we crossed the First Ridge, the engine coughed and spit; we turned around and landed—a flight to nowhere. I remember thinking: my first flight—what am I in for?

Two days later I had my first complete flight over the Hump, this one to Kunming, the main eastern terminus, in southwest China. Round-trip time was seven hours, ten minutes, all but one hour on instruments. It might as well have been all instruments, for above the cloud cover at 18,500 feet, we had no contact with the ground.

It wasn't until three flights later that I got my first glimpse of the Hump. Sheer, absolute beauty—gray cliffs, some variegated in black, most topped by snow-capped peaks. I will never forget that view.

Even on the clearest day, passengers flying the Hump to China in 1944 might have been anxious, for the terrain below, if they saw it, was hostile, to say the least. The 7,000-foot First Ridge and the lush, green carpet of the northern tip of Burma looked deceptively benign compared with the harsh, sheer mountain cliffs still to come farther east, particularly the 15,000-ft Santsung Range between the Salween and Mekong rivers. Fear struck passengers when they realized there'd be no place to land in an emergency, and bailing out was a frightening option. Jump into the dense jungle of Burma (a huge field of broccoli came to mind every time I saw it) and you'd be caught in the top of a 100-foot tree; bail out over the Hump's rugged peaks and you'd be looking at serious injury—or death!

The weather on the Hump was often violent. And unpredictable, requiring the pilot to make decisions about adjusting for changes in winds aloft, about coping with ice. Hump weather was divided into two halves. The monsoon wind of spring and summer brought with it constant heavy rain, (100 inches each month in July and August) in Assam Province where the cluster of Sookerating, Chabua, and Mohanbari bases was located. Life on the ground was miserable. Every surface not covered by concrete or macadam was soggy and muddy, a sea of goo. We looked forward to the fall and winter when the monsoon took its leave and the weather became clearer, drier, and cooler, making life bearable again.

Clouds in the monsoon season were mainly stratus, a gigantic lid covering the Assam valley. Taking off into a blue sky during the spring and summer was a rarity. While there was always weather during the monsoon season requiring instrument flying, negotiating the horizontal stratus clouds was not usually troublesome. Ice was the major problem. But at times, extreme heat rising from the jungles changed monsoon stratus into cumulus or cumulonimbus, causing turbulent and at times indescribably violent thunderstorms. Think of the fiercest storm (not including a hurricane) you can ever recall on the ground, then multiply by 10.

The C-46 is dwarfed by the awesome peaks of the Himalayas.

Clouds in late fall and winter, the monsoon's off-season, were cumulus, not stratus. Free of the boring overcast, the winter Hump was a magnificent kaleidoscope of fair-weather cumulus. Off in the distance on every fall/winter flight, fortunately not always directly on our routes, was the king of the beasts, the towering cumulonimbus, the mightiest rising to over 40,000 feet. Fly through one and you earn your wings. But summer or winter, spring or fall, 996 and all of us faced a potpourri of weather challenges—strong winds, violent storms, wind shear, ice on the wings and all surfaces, ice in the carburetors, near-zero visibility, downdrafts, heavy rain, snow, sleet.

The source of the Hump's violent weather was a confluence of three turbulent air masses—low pressure from the west moving along the main Himalayan ranges; warm, wet high pressure from the Bay of Bengal; cold low pressure from Siberia. On January 6, 1945, these three culprits conspired to serve up the perfect storm, the worst day ever on the Hump, probably the worst day the Air Force has ever flown in.

I rose early that morning for a 0700 takeoff. Our C-46 was 018. The sky looked somehow different from other days, a gun-metal gray lid tightly covering the base. Still not enough time logged to check out as first pilot, I flew copilot for Capt Henry. Hit by severe turbulence on takeoff, we struggled to reach 10,000 feet over Moran, both of us fighting the control columns. The needle on the Automatic Direction Finder spun like a roulette wheel. We knew we were in for more trouble than we'd ever flown in before. Did anyone on the ground—anyone in command, in operations, in the weather service— did anyone know how violent the Hump was that morning?

Capt Otha C. Spencer arrived in Barrackpore, India, in October, 1944, with other pilots of the 10th Weather Squadron. Flying radar-equipped B-25s, their mission was to fly weather route reconnaissance from Barrackpore to Kunming and synoptic flights over the Indian Ocean and the stormy Bay of Bengal. Why didn't the Weather Squadron warn us about the severest conditions ever that day? Because they didn't know. Their modus operandi was to fly few reconnaissance flights over the Hump but daily synoptic flights over the Bay of Bengal and beyond. Col Thomas Hardin, Hump CO, considered the weather service wholly unsatisfactory and issued a remarkable decree: "There is no weather on the Hump." So even if the weather service had known, Capt Henry and I would have nevertheless been in extreme peril over the Hump that terrible day.

We finally reached 10,000 feet and headed east. Rain and sleet hit the fuselage so hard we had to shout to be heard. We hit a wall of even heavier rain, jolting us back in our seats. Ice formed on the wings and the props. When the right engine coughed, we put on carburetor heat. I strapped on my chute. We tuned in our first radio checkpoint, Shingbwiyang, Burma, normally about 40 miles off our left wingtip. The ADF needle swung wildly. I reached up to the ceiling and turned the radio dial to take an "aural null." We were dumfounded—we were right over the beacon, 40 miles north of our course! Capt Henry watched intently. Realizing the wind was coming not from the west, its prevailing direction, but from the south at over 100 mph, we threw the plane sharply right, making a huge correction of 30 degrees into the wind. We crabbed sideways to Paoshan, China.

The turbulence grew worse. Hail like golf balls struck the fuselage. The radio operator stuck his head into the cockpit and told us he'd heard five planes on Mayday reporting lost engines, seeking a fix, preparing to bail out. We crossed over Paoshan and changed course to 120 degrees, maintaining that unheard-of 30-degree correction. The leg from Paoshan to Kunming, we knew, would be longer than the normal 45 minutes. We told ourselves, make it to Kunming, then a 10-minute flight northeast to Chanyi, our destination, and we'd remain overnight. Certainly by this time the Hump would be closed.

Wrong! Gen William Tunner, who had taken over as CO five months earlier, changed Col Hardin's "There is no weather on the Hump" to an even more direct and stunning edict: "The Hump is never closed." At Hump Pilot Association reunions long afterward I was incredulous when I heard pilots reminiscing about "the night the Hump was closed." Closed? Really? In his book Over the Hump *Gen Tunner said he issued an order "to the effect that weather was a factor which every Operations Officer would consider in dispatching aircraft." Really? We never knew that. In Chanyi, China, that day, we pleaded to remain overnight but were told Chanyi had no authority to suspend operations. To avoid returning to India, some crews submitted false Form 1 Maintenance Reports, claiming mechanical problems. Capt Henry and I never considered that ruse. We boarded 018 and headed back through hell.*

Eighteen pilots and crewmen who flew on January 6, 1945, wrote to me about their scary flights. (See my Tales of the Himalayas.*)*

> ➢ *Ken Jolly (Owensboro, KY): "We could not maintain our assigned altitude of 16,500 feet. We had such heavy ice that if we wanted to climb, the plane burbled for a stall."*
> ➢ *Bill Hanahan (Phoenix, AZ): "As we flew over Burma we were tossed about violently. Propeller ice released by the alcohol de-icers sounded like bullets as it hit the fuselage. It took both Capt Downie and me on the control columns to maintain a level attitude."*

106

➤ *J. V. Vinyard (Amarillo, TX): "Static electricity built up on our aircraft, smothering all radio homing facility. I tried a homing station to the north of our route. By good fortune we were directly over it: we had been blown 65 miles north of course!"*

➤ *Bill Watts (Tuscon, AZ): "I flew out of Misamari the famous January 6 day. Our field lost three planes."*

➤ *Bill Sackett (Haskell, NJ): "Flying C-46 with Troop Carrier, I too was in that fierce January storm."*

➤ *Col Jack Tamm, Retired (Daytona, FL): "Like you, I made 96 round-trips on the Hump, including the January 6, 1945, trip. My return cargo that day consisted of young Chinese men destined to be trained as pilots in the USA. What an indoctrination flight for them."*

➤ *John Meek (Ketchum, OK): "A civilian pilot, I was recruited by the Army, eventually flying C-46s out of Tezgaon. I too flew in that storm."*

➤ *Don Bean (Portland, OR): "I flew out of Sookerating and remember well the January storm."*

➤ *John Wilson, Capt, EAL, Ret. (Sanbornton, NH): "I remember well the weather of the January 6 storm. We beat it back to Jorhat on the fifth and reported it".*

➤ *Jay Warner (Rochester, NY): "I recall the storm of January 6. A few Chabua guys came back after throwing out their cargos. Said they were blown on top. Incidentally, I topped you by three trips. I had 99 before going to Gaya to instruct."*

➤ *Nelson Beck (North Warren, PA): "A radio operator on C-46s, I ended up with 809 hours and over 100 missions. I was on a two-day mission a day before January 6. Lucky!"*

➤ *Jim Calvert (San Antonio, TX): "I was operations officer the night of the big storm. The crews that came in that night were physically and emotionally shook up."*

➢ *Howard Randol (Capistrano, CA) "I arrived in Misamari the day after the big storm. We lost eight planes."*

➢ *Tom Manning (Higden, AZ): "On January 6 the wind was out of the south at 110. I carried a 45-degree correction and was an hour and a half overdue reaching Kunming. I made 85 round-trips, none worse than that one."*

➢ *Lt Col Jack Pipkin (Vacaville, CA): "I landed at your field of Chabua a few times during my tour in India. My most memorable landing there was an emergency when I was low on gas after flying through the granddaddy of all storms."*

➢ *Col Jean Nutty (Oklahoma City, OK): "I also flew the night of the Big Storm. One thing about flying the Hump—you came back a much better pilot. It's not too surprising we never met, for there wasn't much time for socializing."*

➢ *Bob Van Buskirk (Aurora, CO): "Our C-54 got kicked around the night of January 6. But that was tolerable—until #3 engine came unglued. We made it into the RAF base at Sylhet. (C-54 pilot called the Lord for help. The Lord came back: 'Son, I'm so busy with those poor C-46 and CNAC boys, you four-engine guys are on your own.' ")*

➢ *Ed Randell (Cameron Park, CA): "On January 6 I flew a C-87 from Jorhat to China and back. On the return flight we were blown north off course toward Tibet and were low on fuel. After getting a radio fix from Calcutta, we headed for Tezpur for fuel. After we broke out of the clouds, I saw a mountain dead ahead. I told the weather officer at Jorhat that we had winds nearly 200 mph. His reply: 'The wind never blows that hard.' "*

Some crews bailed out that day, some lost an engine. All flew through the most severe turbulence, ice and hail ever. All cringed but made the biggest correction into the wind they had ever made in their flying careers. Without that correction, they would have joined the doomed crews blown into the 20,000-plus-foot peaks of the Himalayas in the north, cousins of mighty Mt. Everest.

Estimates of losses in that 24-hour period vary. From my knowledge at the base and my reading after the war, I estimate the Hump lost 15 planes and crews—from ATC, Troop Carrier, Combat Cargo transport commands; from fighter/bomber commands; and from CNAC transport operations.

How sad that the Air Transport Command apparently did not believe—or chose to ignore—the dire reports of their own crews that day. How sad that a macho edict stood in the way of reason.

Chapter 13

The Commander Signs Off

Three days before leaving for Beijing to begin the Damnya mission, Capt Kent made a final validation presentation to the Commander, Maj Gen Winfield and staff officers. Assisting Capt Kent were Dr. Tyrell, anthropologist and recovery leader, Mark Gilbertson, mountaineer, and SSG Beemster, mountaineer. The captain began by reviewing the discovery of the CH-00628 site by Tibetan hunters, verification of Missing Aircraft 9675 at that site, general description of the site on a mountain slope of 35-40 degrees, task organization, training objectives, risk mitigation, and Tibet Operation timetable.

The substance of the briefing was a report on pre-deployment mountain training of the staff from 10 – 27 June at the Black Rapids Site and at Denali National Park in Alaska. The training event was prepared and conducted by skilled mountaineers of the Northern War Training Center, Fort Wainright, Alaska. Objectives were to learn fundamental mountaineering skills; to become familiar with equipment; to simulate terrain, distance, and hazards in movement; to work effectively in high altitude; to be eligible for fitness and mission validation. Team members were trained in specific skills:

- ✓ Identifying, using, maintaining equipment
- ✓ Planning hikes
- ✓ Setting up camps
- ✓ Sustaining field water
- ✓ Planning and packaging food
- ✓ Preventing injury
- ✓ Traveling and climbing in snow
- ✓ Expedition climbing
- ✓ Climbing rocks
- ✓ Handling rope and communication
- ✓ Employing belay devices and techniques
- ✓ Rappelling
- ✓ Crossing rivers
- ✓ Employing rope bridges
- ✓ Rescuing by MEDEVAC and crevasse rescue
- ✓ Learning mountain geology
- ✓ Being aware of altitude illness
- ✓ Mountaineering Leadership
- ✓ Functioning in cold weather

Capt Kent and his staff displayed 50 Alaska photographs showing all aspects of the team's training, including Triathlon, "self-arrest," arrival at summit of Gunny Sack I, moving on difficult terrain (schist rock, mica, silt), setting up camps, ascents, at Windy Corner, and at Motorcycle Hill. Gen Winfield was impressed with the success of the training and appreciative of the thorough presentation. Capt Kent credited the success to the strong support from the Command, enthusiastic involvement of the augmentees, and first-rate work of the Northern Warfare Training Center personnel. He also pointed to early planning and coordination, good equipment, and physical preparedness. The briefing ended with a preview of military and commercial flights during deployment and redeployment to Beijing, Lhasa, Osan Air Base (Republic of Korea), and Hickam AFB.

In closing, Capt Kent said, "Team Tibet is prepared to successfully conduct the Tibet mission." Gen Winfield agreed. He gave the team members a thumbs-up, wished them well, and sent them on their way.

Chapter 14

Team Physician

Maj Karl Larsen is one of five "augmentees" asked by Capt Kent to supplement the JPAC cadre on the 2004 Tibet mission. The major's one-word response to the invitation was a quick, "Absolutely!"

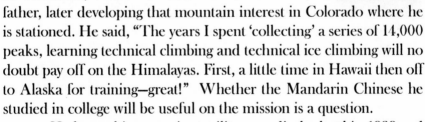

Karl Larsen is a medical doctor. He grew up in California, where he hiked the Sierras with his father, later developing that mountain interest in Colorado where he is stationed. He said, "The years I spent 'collecting' a series of 14,000 peaks, learning technical climbing and technical ice climbing will no doubt pay off on the Himalayas. First, a little time in Hawaii then off to Alaska for training—great!" Whether the Mandarin Chinese he studied in college will be useful on the mission is a question.

He began his career in a military medical school in 1989 and took his regular commission when he graduated in 1993. He then did a year of surgical training and became Flight Surgeon for the Special Operations Command. Stationed in England for three years, he deployed to remote sites frequently for fieldwork in Africa, Bosnia, and Eastern Europe.

After he returned stateside, he went to San Antonia, Texas, to train in orthopedic surgery. He finishing his residency in 2001 then went on to Indianapolis for sub-specialty training in hand and micro-vascular surgery. He moved next to the Air Force Academy in Colorado Springs, his current station, where he is chief of orthopedic surgery. His partner there had been on the 2002 mission to recover four crewmen of a Hump C-46 in Tibet; his enthusiasm for the experience played a big part in Karl's prompt acceptance of the invitation.

A major concern of Dr. Larsen is medical evacuation. The procedure is clear and spelled out, and the mission will be well equipped for emergencies, but the risk would be lessened significantly if the Chinese government allowed for the use of a helicopter, he said.

Even though the Daymna crash site is at 14,100 feet, the team will not use oxygen. Before they leave for the site, the team will spend a week in and around Lhasa acclimatizing themselves to altitude, training their bodies to tolerate the dizzying heights. Most mountaineers, he explained, do not require oxygen until they get to about 25,000 feet. Some climbers who scale fabled Everest, which is about 400 miles southwest of Damnya, need oxygen, some do not. Those who don't are rare indeed.

In spite of the altitude of the crash site, bodies of the three airmen are completely decomposed, Dr. Larsen said. He and every team member will pitch in, searching for bone and material and artifacts under the direction of Dr. Tyrell, recovery leader.

Karl and his wife have two sons, 3 and 7. The 7-year-old is keen on learning as much as he can about his dad's first MIA adventure on the other side of the globe. It will be good stuff for "show and tell" in school. The major's family, as well as his wife's family, especially her grandfather, were also into the experience. Grandfather was a B-24 pilot. "Colonel Buck likes to talk about it, he said," with a grin.

Like Dr. Tyrell, Maj Larsen is fortunate to be able to merge his avocation of climbing with his professional specialty.

Chapter 15

Next Stop—Tibet!

8 August. The final phase of team preparations before deployment was complete. Satisfied that things were looking good, getting a thumbs-up in a final briefing for the commander, Capt Kent flew to Beijing, taking with him SFC Swam, Dr. Tyrell, and GySgt Behn. They then flew on to Pyongyang, North Korea, to expedite the shipping of equipment used in a just-completed JPAC recovery mission. The four then returned to Beijing.

11 August, Beijing, Kerry Center Hotel, Beijing. Capt Kent sent a Situation Report (SITREP) to JPAC Command concerning activities and needs. In the morning he and his cadre briefed Rear Admiral Mauldin in his Defense Attachment Office on the recovery mission. In the afternoon they briefed Ambassador Randt. Both were very supportive of JPAC and the mission.

Capt Kent reported that the Defense Attachment Office supports conducting repatriation ceremonies in Beijing if the mission is successful in recovering remains. Adm Mauldin requested information on the conduct of a repatriation ceremony in a host country. Capt Kent asked that information on this be sent to him before he leaves for Tibet. He added the need for a point of contact at JPAC who could coordinate with the Embassy as the team gets into October and closer to the end of the mission. Capt Kent asked the Command to forward a copy of the JPAC press release to the Beijing

Public Affairs Office of the U.S. embassy in Beijing. He added that the PAO here is requesting guidance from JPAC's Public Affairs Office on dealing with media, particularly the Chinese media.

Equipment cleared customs and was shipped to Lhasa, received by the Tibetan Ministry of Foreign Affairs and staged at their office awaiting arrival of team.

Delays by the MFA have the JPAC team arriving in Lhasa on 17 August, three days after negotiated date. No issue here; will readjust schedule. Will start movement to site only after team has acclimated.

Team will be escorted into Tibet by Embassy personnel: Adm Mauldin, DAO Marine Attache Maj Riva, POL/MIL Officer Mr. Plant.

Next 24/48/72: Will continue coordination with the Defense Attachment Office and Tibetan Military Foreign Affairs, specifically on air transportation and team clearance to enter Tibet. Preparing to receive remainder of team on 13 August.

13 August SITREP, Kerry Center Hotel, Beijing. The team was issued clearance to enter Tibet and tickets for air travel on 17 August. The main body of the team arrived in Beijing this evening. No major issues with customs, but some frustrations. Last-minute clearances, intentional delays in schedule are seemingly modus operandi. Little impact on mission execution. Satellite communication, medical equipment, and narcotics have cleared and remain in possession of the recovery team.

16 August SITREP, Kerry Center Hotel, Beijing. Team started pre-medication on Diamox for acclimatization period, which begins tomorrow with the team's departure from Beijing and arrival in Lhasa, Tibet. The team is expected to arrive at approximately 2100 hours.

Next 24/48/72: Acclimatization

17 August SITREP, Lhasa Hotel, Lhasa. Traveling with the DATT, his Marine Attache, the Embassy POL/MIL, and Beijing

Liaison Officer, the team arrived in Lhasa and was greeted by local officials and transported to hotel. The team will attend a banquet hosted by the Ministry of Foreign Affairs. There were again positive comments on data transfer from Tibet with INMARSAT. Elevation in Lhasa—team reports no issues with Acute Mountain Sickness. RFI (Request for Information): Require information paper of in-country repatriation ceremony.

Next 24/48/72: Meeting to set schedule and make final coordination, inspect and account for prepositioned equipment, acclimatize.

<u>18 August SITREP, Lhasa Hotel, Lhasa.</u> Team Leader attended meeting with Deputy Director-General of the Foreign Affairs Office of the Tibetan Autonomous District for modifications and final budget agreement. The team attended a banquet hosted by the Director-General. Because the arrival of the team had been delayed—Tibetan holidays, PRC officials, and late payment of advance (no fault of JPAC)—a modified schedule was agreed to in order to ensure Chinese team's preparation. Arrival at the crash site will be on September 1, two days later than initially planned. Some joint training and preparations were cut short.

New schedule:
<u>19 August</u> - continued adaptation to climate
<u>20 August</u> - team access and inspection of equipment; joint mountain training at the Mountaineering Association of TAR
<u>21 August</u>- AM: Chinese preparations; PM: Joint physical training and joint mountain training
<u>22 August</u> – AM: visit Potala Palace; PM: horse-handling (not to be confused with horse-riding)
<u>23-24 August</u> - Equipment loading, distribution and preparations, mainly of Chinese team
<u>25 August</u> - Drive to Bayi Town; Remain over night
<u>26 August</u> – Meetings with local officials; RON
<u>27 August</u>- Drive to Damnya Village; RON

28 August– Hire local labor, pack animals; prepare equipment for carry
29 August- (AM) Continue preparations; SP for crash site; (PM) Camp 1
29 – 1 September- Move toward crash site

Chinese team has agreed to participate in recovery effort itself under the direction of Dr. Tyrell.

20 August SITREP, Lhasa Hotel, Lhasa. The team had access to its equipment. Everything accounted for. The JPAC and Chinese teams conducted joint training at the Tibetan Mountaineering Guide School. The Defense Office Attache leaves tomorrow. He asked for the information about in-country repatriation service. The team leader needs this in the morning. The Chinese are supportive of the service, preferring it be held in Lhasa. The DOA said it is likely to be held in Beijing. JPAC Liaison Officer leaves Lhasa on 22 August. Defense Attache Office representative remains at the Joint Office at the Lhasa Hotel throughout the mission. The following communication systems are positive: Iridium, Email, WW Cell, INMARSAT, Pager. There has been one case of stomach flu due to diet change. There have been no problems with altitude sickness. Dr. Larsen celebrated his 37th birthday.
Next 24/48/72: 21 August – (AM) Chinese preparations; (PM) Joint mountain training and physical training. 22 August – (AM) Potala Palace; (PM) Horse-handling

21-22-23 August SITREP, Lhasa Hotel, Lhasa. 21 August: The team conducted joint training with the Chinese team at the Tibetan Mountaineering Guide School. For the Chinese team, training and participation were limited. The Defense Attache left. 22 August: Team toured the Potala Palace in the morning and participated in horse-handling training in the afternoon. Plans and Operations relayed that repatriation ceremony information will be provided the Defense Attaches Office early this week. JPAC Liaison Officer left. The Chinese team leader refused to acknowledge the February transportation agreement. Could be a sticking point in final negotiations at end of mission. With the backing of the U.S. Embassy, JPAC will hold firm on the 4 February agreement. The team inspected the Chinese team equipment; were pleased to find that the PRC team had purchased all necessary and agreed-to equipment. Equipment of the Chinese team was prepared, distributed, and uploaded. Equipment of the U.S. team was uploaded into equipment trucks.

<u>24 August SITREP, Lhasa Hotel, Lhasa.</u> The team departs tomorrow for Bayi Town, driving time approximately 6 hours.

Chapter 16

Team Tibet Deploys to Crash Site

Captain Kent Sends Situation Reports
to JPAC Command

Day 1

25 August 2004
Bayi Town - Lin Zhi Hotel
N 29 40' 0 .59"; E 94 21' 49.2"

We departed Lhasa at 0800 hours and arrived in Bayi Town at 1600 hours. The drop in elevation was from 12,100 feet in Lhasa to 10,400 feet in Bayi, with a 16,400-foot climb en route. The transport was by two-lane hard surface the entire route.   ≈ The team remains healthy.   ≈ All equipment and the Chinese team, 22 persons including Mr. Ju, Deputy Director of the Foreign Affairs Office of the Tibet Autonomous Region, were also in Bayi.   ≈ Next 24/48/72: 26 August – meet with local officials; purchase fuel; 27 August – Depart for Damnya Village; 28 August – final equipment preparation.

CFC: En route to and from the crash site, Capt Kent e-mailed me copies of daily Situation Reports (SITREPS) he sent to the JPAC Command in Honolulu. To make theses military reports reader-friendly,

I have paraphrased them into civilian style. After the team completed its mission and returned to Hickam AFB, the captain sent me excerpts from the personal journal he wrote on the mission. The excerpts make up Chapter 18.

Capt. Kent (third from left) and Sgt. Swam (far right) join Nyingzhi Prefecture officials in a toast to a successful mission on the mountain.

At another table, Team Tibet 2004 members join in the toast.

Day 2
26 August
Bayi Town
73 degrees, cloudy, light rain

We met with the Executive Deputy Commissioner for Nyingzhi Prefecture, Mr. Shi Wen. The purpose of the meeting was for prefecture officials and Peoples Liberation Army officers to become acquainted with the joint China-U.S. MIA team. Mr. Shi briefed the joint team on the geographic and cultural details of the prefecture. He stated that Bayi Town was the economic and cultural center of the prefecture and that heavy investment by the Central Government put into the Nyingzhi Prefecture had resulted in improvement of its infrastructure, economic growth, and social progress. Mr. Shi concluded by concurring with earlier views expressed in Beijing and Lhasa—that the mission will play a positive role in promoting mutual understanding between PRC and US in boosting bilateral exchanges. ≈ In the evening we attended a banquet at the Linghzi Hotel hosted by Mr. Liu Laixing, Deputy Commissioner of the prefecture. Noting the success of the 2002 mission that also took place in the prefecture, he pledged complete cooperation of the people of Nyingzhi on this mission.

Day 3
27 August
Damnya Village, Milin County, Nyingzhi Prefecture
N 29 26' 29.6"; E 94 42' 40.9"
73 degrees; mostly cloudy, light rain

The U.S. and Chinese teams departed Bayi Town at 0830 hours and arrived at Damnya Village at 1130 hours. Both teams made preparations with local labor and prepped and packed equipment for carry. ≈ The team remains healthy. Cooperation with the Chinese team since leaving Lhasa is excellent. ≈ Next 24/48/72: 28 August – Final equipment preparation; 29 August – Depart for camp 1 on 30 August – continue to camp 2

Linguist Ng converses with Chinese general at the dinner.

Chinese and U.S. teams relaxing after excavation.

Day 4
28 August
Damnya Village
73 degrees; mostly cloudy, light rain

Final preparations. We packed equipment for movement after prioritizing it for carry by local labor and pack animals. The team conducted training with the Portable Altitude Chamber and the Kendricks Extraction Device (Skedco Stretcher). ≈ The team conducted map reconnaissance and verified the route with the Chinese team leader. We will follow the route as briefed in Hawaii. ≈ We attended a dinner with local village officials. ≈ We will depart tomorrow morning for Camp 1.

Day 5
29 August
August 29 Camp 1, Elevation 11,500 feet
N 29 18' 40.7; E 94 48' 27.
50 degrees, cloudy, rain

We departed Damnya Village at 1030 hours after loading equipment onto pack animals. We moved 16 km, ascended 1,800 feet, arrived at 1645 hours, and established our first camp at the base of a mountain in a high altitude cloud forest.

The route to Camp 1:

SP	N 29 26' 29.9"	E 94 42' 39.7"
:30	N 29 25' 42.8"	E 94 43' 54":
60	N 29 24' 49.5"	E 94 44' 34.8"
:90	N 29 23' 48.0"	E 94 45' 08.1"
2:00	N 29 22' 52.9"	E 94 45' 44"
2:30	N 29 22' 49.6"	E 94 46' 08"
3:00	N 29 21' 57.2"	E 94 46' 43.8"
3:30	N 29 21' 29.7"	E 94 47' 01"

Camp 1 N 29 20' 57.9 E 94 47' 13.1" (Horse drop-off)

Until they reached their drop-off point at the river, pack horses from Bayi Town took the heaviest burden off porters.

Photo by Dr. Tyrell

Every journey starts with a single step. The men are clean as a whistle and eager to get going as they leave the village of Damnya and civilization itself behind.

Day 6
30 August
Camp 2, Elevation 11,500 feet
N 29 18' 40.7"; E 94 48' 27.2'
50 degrees, cloudy, rain

We departed Camp 1 at 0830 hours, climbed to 14,800 feet, crossed Damnya Mountain, descended to 11,500 feet and arrived at Camp 2 at 2230 hours. Conditions on the trail were wet with limited visibility. The trail was very difficult, particularly when combined with oxygen deprivation. The Chinese doctor was diagnosed with a respiratory infection and potentially High Altitude Pulmonary Edema (HAPE) due to poor adjustment to altitude at Camp 1. He returned to Damnya and will likely meet up with the team in about a week. The U.S. team had some reaction to the movement at altitude when crossing Damnya Mountain at 14,800 feet, resulting in three cases of Acute Mountain sickness (AMS). All symptoms subsided upon descent to below 13, 500 feet and after treatment by Dr. Larsen.

The route to Camp 2:

SP	N 29 20' 57.9"	E 94 47' 13.1"
2:00	N 29 20' 40.9"	E 94 47' 22.4"
4:00	N 29 20' 10.7"	E 94 47' 25.3"
6:00	N 29 19' 45.6"	E 94 47' 32.3" (14,800 feet)
7:00	N 29 19' 24.1"	E 94 47' 34.2"
9:00	N 29 19' 16.8"	E 94 47' 53.2"
10:00	N 29 19" 05.5"	E 94 47' 57.9"
11:00	N 29 18' 55.3"	E 94 48' 12.3"
13:00	N 29 18' 40.7"	E 94 48' 27.2" (Camp 2)

Day 7
31 August
Camp 2

We spent the day resting and refitting to ensure no further health problems prior to tomorrow's move to Camp 3.

Heading out on the initial climb to cross the 14,800-foot Damnya Mountain. The backpack weighed 60 pounds, but soaked by rain, It was more like 100.

Photo by Mike Harris

Andy Tyrell at ease in camp 1 at the base of a high mountain. Behind him is a "forest of clouds", a high altitude rain forest.

The river we had to cross was deeper than anticipated, approximately 5.5 feet, and moving at high speed, with white water. Camp 2 was located in a deep valley boxed in by peaks 14,000 to 17,000 feet high. We were surrounded by dozen of waterfalls in these mountains. They feed directly into the river we must cross. Mountaineers Gilbertson and Beemster installed a two-rope bridge from one river bank to the other. It took all day for the U.S. team, the Chinese team, and 60 porters plus equipment to cross the river safely. ≈ We established Camp 3 on the other side of the river at N 29 18' 3.7"; E 94 48' 27.5" at altitude 11,500 feet.   ≈ We are obviously still right in the middle of the rainy season. The rain has refused to let up.

CFC: The monsoon is a six-month natural phenomenon. It comes in spring and lasts through autumn. In another few weeks it will be gone.

Photo by Dr. Tyrell

After a long night of walking, the team arrived at camp 2. The next day was a day of rest. As the men moved out and prepared to cross the river the following morning, they enjoyed sensational views of waterfalls cascading from high mountain peaks.

It took all day to get the contingent of 96 men across the river. U.S. and Chinese mountaineers drilled anchors into rocks and ran ropes across the fast-moving white water. Earlier in the day, when the river was lower, the Chinese team leader and Mountaineer Gilbertson walked arm-in-arm across the river to pull the ropes across. Direction of travel was from right to left.

Photo by Mike Harris

Mike Swam pulled across a turbulent, rain-swollen river via ropes.

Day 9
2 September
Camp 4, Elevation 12,500 feet
N 29 16' 28" E 94 48' 18.5
50 degrees, cloudy, rain

The movement to Camp 4 was a grueling nine-hour hike, aggravated by continuous rain. The mountaineers had to fix a hand line over one steep pass. One team member developed a moderate case of Acute Mountain Sickness as we approached 13,500 feet. He was assisted over the pass at 14,600 feet, and all symptoms subsided as we approached Camp 4 at 12,500 feet.

The route to Camp 4:
SP	N 29 18' 32.7" E 94 48' 27.5" (Camp 3)	
1:30	N 29 18' 11.2" E 94 48' 42.8"	
3:30	N 29 17' 28.0" E 94 49' 04.6"	
4:50	N 29 17' 12.2" E 94 49' 15.6"	
7:00	N 29 16' 47.1" E 94 49' 05.1" (14,600-ft pass)	
8:20	N 29 16' 30.3" E 94 48' 38.0"	
9:10	N 29 16' 28.0" E 94 48' 18.5" Camp 4, 12,500 feet	

Day 10
3 September
Camp 4

Camp 4 is located 1,700 feet directly below the crash site. From our camp we can look up and see portions of airplane wreckage that has moved down the slope over time due to glacier melting and gravitational pull.

A tough but picturesque climb in the rain on the day after the
river-crossing. The two mountaineers left early that morning
to put in guide lines at precarious places.

Photo by Mike Haris

With team photographer Morales leading the way, the men
negotiated a narrow ledge along a precipice. The guide lines
were installed by Mountaineer Gilbertson.

The team negotiates a perilous passage.

Pausing to take in the magnificent scenery, team members look down the valley and beyond to their next obstacle.

The peak in the background is in India. Camp 3 at bottom right soon became engulfed by a huge cloud.

After climbing the second mountain, the team set up camp 3. The team will remain a couple days before tackling the final push to the crash site. For the 13-member team there were six 2-man tents and one single.

We will remain at camp 4 for at least two more nights in order to ensure proper team acclimatization. We have only one member we have concerns about. All others have no issues with altitude above 14,500 feet. After medication and treatment by Dr. Larsen, we anticipate that all will be ready to move to the crash site after the rest period.   ≈ We established an area for the final camp 100 feet above the crash site. I conducted a reconnaissance of the crash site.   ≈ Dr. Tyrell, Recovery Leader, conducted an initial survey of the crash site. He reported that the site is on a 35-45 degree slope. Natural movement has therefore spread debris hundreds of meters down the slope, even lower in the course of two years since a four-man party from the 2002 Rouse team investigated the site. A concentration of wreckage and debris remains at the point of the plane's impact. Dr. Tyrell determined a 30m x 40m initial project area, with the possibility of expansion. It will be impossible for us to complete the project within the constraints of time and weather. However, over the next couple weeks we should complete the impact area, and within 30 days should complete the initial project area. We plan to move out of the area no later than 1 October, when winter weather is expected. The next 10-15 days should tell us a lot.   ≈ In the impact area Andy and I spotted a number of cockpit and life support items on the surface, but no remains.

The route to crash site:

SP	N 29 16' 28.0"	E 94 48' 18.5" (Camp 4)
:15	N 29 16' 27.6"	E 94 48' 13.2"
:35	N 29 16' 40.6"	E 94 48' 07.5"
1:05	N 29 16' 47.2"	E 94 48' 09.0"
1:40	N 29 16' 52.4	E 94 48' 14.6"
:20	N 29 16' 54.6"	E 94 48' 13.8" (Crash site)
:20	N 29 16' 55.7"	E 94 48' 12.0" (Final camp site)

(Crash site–14,200 feet; Final camp –14,300)

Maj. Larsen, team doctor, tending to an injured finger.

The push to reach the crash site and set up the fifth and final camp.

Day 11
4 September
Crash Site (Final) Base Camp

Today is the seventh day of continuous rain. We prepped and pushed equipment up to Final Base Camp. Dr. Tyrell, Recovery Leader, formulated excavation strategy and plan. The team remains at Camp 4. The Chinese team reconnoiters for a camp site closer to the crash site. The Chinese team is slow to move because of the weather, but they are very supportive of our requests. They are certainly eager to have this project finished as soon as possible. The local labor is amazingly resilient and tough.

Day 12
5 September
Crash Site
N 29 16' 54.6" E 94 48' 13.8"
14,100 feet

The team moved up to the crash site and established the Final Base Camp. The crash site was set up for excavation to begin on 6 September. There have been no issues with acclimatization other than simply less oxygen with which to work. Dr. Larsen had infections in two fingers of this left hand. With the assistance of Rocky Keohuhu-Bolor, team medic, he performed surgery on himself and is recovering fine.

As the team approaches the GPS
coordinates of the crash site, this
spectacular view greets them.

The crash site closer now, it is still spectacular.

Day 13
6 September
Crash Site Base Camp

Having set up the Crash Site Base Camp, today we began excavating the site, sorting through large rocks and wreckage beneath what is believed to be the left wing of the C-46. Recovery Leader Tyrell can clearly identify the point of impact and the direction of flight (north). The three 3m x 3m grid units we excavated yielded only a piece of a flashlight.   ≈ The Chinese team members came up from their campsite 1,500 feet below. They informed us that re-supply of food and fuel and non-essential comfort items would arrive at our base camp in two days.   ≈ In spite of this being the ninth day of continuous rainfall, team members remain healthy and motivated.

CFC: Every team member participates in the physical work of excavation. JPAC's eBrochure describes it as "physically painstaking, sweaty, arduous, and meticulous."

Stationed at Chabua, India, 133 miles south of the crash site, I endured the same miserable rainy weather, 100 inches of rain a month in July and August. But as I recall, the six-month monsoon left sometime in September.

I gulped when I read that the plane's direction when it crashed was NORTH. If the crew realized they had overshot their destination of Sookerating, India, on their westerly flight from China and were turning around, a turn to the south, away from the highest mountains, would have been standard.

Photo by Mike Harris

Folded hills behind him, the big one in the distance in India, Alfred Castro surveys the crash on the first day of excavation.

Mountain climbing and excavating are not enough exercise for some team members. Here is Gabe Serna using elastic cords anchored in rock.

Day 14
7 September
Crash Site

Excavation work continued. We completed the excavation of three 3m x 3m grids and two grids are in progress. The excavation included moving heavy rocks and wreckage of various sizes and careful excavation of soil beneath the wreckage to the bedrock of the mountain. Significant items found include a piece of nylon material, a piece of cloth probably from a shirt, another piece of flashlight, and a single strand of hair ginger/red in color wedged in a piece of wreckage. This supports Recovery Leader Tyrell's theory that the crew did not bail out and in fact crashed with the aircraft.   Mountaineer Gilbertson slipped and sliced open his right thumb at its base near the palm. Team Medic Keohuhu-Bolor irrigated the wound with sterile water and stitched it with six sutures. Dr. Larsen determined that despite the deep cut there was no damage to the nerves or tendons. ≈ Along with local labor, the Chinese team provided a great deal of assistance on site, a big boost to our day's production.

CFC: On September 7 I flew to Denver for a reunion of the Hump Pilots Association. My feelings were mixed—I looked forward to the reunion and to our presenting a one-sixth bronze scale model C-46 to the Air Force Academy at Colorado Springs. But I was anxious to stay with Team Tibet as they excavate the crash site. I could have taken my laptop to Denver with me but I knew there'd be little time to use it.

Using a transit, Anthropologist Tyrell measures angles to lay out the crash site.

Gary Beemster installs anchors
on cliff for rigging.

As other team members pulled, Mark Gilbertson checked the anchor.

Gilbertson, Beemster, Ng, and Harris pull ropes tight, The rigging was installed to help the team move wreckage for searching.

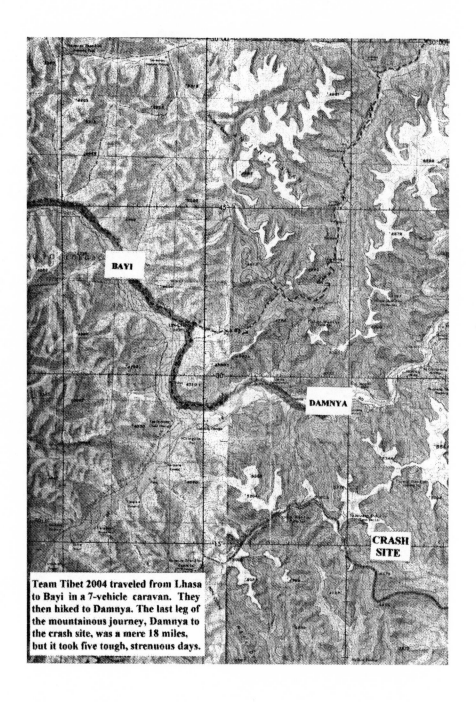

BAYI

DAMNYA

CRASH SITE

Team Tibet 2004 traveled from Lhasa to Bayi in a 7-vehicle caravan. They then hiked to Damnya. The last leg of the mountainous journey, Damnya to the crash site, was a mere 18 miles, but it took five tough, strenuous days.

Day 15
8 September
Crash Site

For the first time in 10 days, we saw the sun this morning. We had a chance to take things out of the tents and dry them before heading down to the crash site. Except for a brief hailstorm in the afternoon, the weather remained partly clear for most of the day. With the help of the Chinese team, we had a very productive day, closing out six grid units. The Chinese team reports that our non-essential comfort items and re-supply of food and fuel will arrive at our base camp tomorrow. Items recovered today include an oxygen mask, an earpiece to a radio headset, and a seat belt that appears to have been ripped from the pilot seat. This is another indicator in support of the Recovery Leader's theory that the crew went down with the aircraft. Mountaineer Gilbertson is doing fine and is in 72 quarters (72 hours rest). The team has acclimatized well and has stopped taking Diamox. There are no health issues.

Day 16
9 September
Crash Site

The team completed six grids. Working around an aircraft wheel, the excavation included moving heavy rocks and wreckage. The only significant item excavated was a piece of an earphone. Excavation is moving quickly. The Chinese team continues to work well and delivered non-essential comfort items and food and fuel as scheduled.

Photo by Dr. Tyrell

Happy day! After 10 days of rain, the sun finally put in an appearance. Everything was hung out to dry at the Kent-Swam "hootch" of many colors.

Marine Lance Corporal Ng at breakfast.

Day 17
10 September
Crash Site

The team completed six grid units, working consistently and moving closer to the right wing and fuselage. Remarkable items recovered were rubber overboot, buttons, and pieces of fabric and leather. Mountaineer Gilbertson will return to the work site tomorrow. There is no infection in his hand. Chinese Team Leader Targa returns to Damnya Village and Bayi tomorrow to handle official business. We will not see him again until exfill (exfiltrate) when we return to Damnya. In the next Sitrep I will provide an estimated closure date and exfill plan.

Day 18
11 September
Crash Site

We excavated five grid units. Significant items recovered include oxygen mask, two pistol belts, gun holster, clothing material that looks like a pant pocket.

Day 19
12 September
Crash Site

We excavated three additional grid units. Significant items recovered include holster for flare pistol, fabric material, webbing, piece of pistol grip (likely from flare gun), and a button. We have not yet recovered remains or personal effects.

Day 20
13 September
Crash Site

We completed two grid units. The team cut into and sorted through wreckage that was believed to be the location of the cockpit.

The sun setting, shadows are long at the crash camp site. The men are relaxing, swapping stories.

Dinner on the Roof of the World. (L to R) Larsen, Tyrell, Swam, Kent, Harris, Behn enjoy Mountain House Dehydrated Meals out of heated pouches. Chicken Terriyaki, spaghetti and meatballs, pot roast —"really pretty good" was Geoff Kent's critique.

Significant items recovered include a custom-made leather pistol belt inscribed with the initial "A", a radio headset, assorted fabric and webbing, pocket of a flight jacket. Given the number of life-support material we have uncovered, we are baffled that we have recovered only one personal effect (custom-made pistol belt) and no remains. Each day, theories such as bail out of the crew increase.

CFC: On the flight home from Denver on September 12, I couldn't escape the uneasy, albeit uninformed, feeling that if the crew went down with the plane, by this time the team should have found at least one piece of bone. The first thing I did when I got into my apartment late that night was rush to the computer and breathlessly scan all the sitreps waiting for me. There were no reports of finding bone.

I wondered about the families. I don't know whether they were aware of the on-going recovery mission, but certainly, if there were family, JPAC would inform them at the conclusion of the mission. If the crew had bailed out, closure had escaped them and their loved ones would remain in JPAC's Missing in Action file. But could they still be alive in Tibet? The new book Lost in Tibet *by Starks and Murcutt narrates the frightening adventures of a Hump crew who bailed out over Tibet a year earlier (1943)...and their amazing good fortune in escaping from that forbidden land.*

Day 21
14 September
Crash Site

We excavated four grid units. Significant items recovered include four buttons, an oxygen mask, lift-the-dot fasteners, a navigation aid and seat belts. ≈ We moved up slope of the impact area and find there is little else to recover. We are moving a lot of rock and screening less and less soil. The team is now working toward scientific and mission completion. We have six grid units remaining then we will dig test pits south of the impact area under the direction of the Recovery Leader.

Gabe Serna examining a piece of the wreckage.

At a screening table, Mike Swam is searching for remains.

Team members Tyrell, Behn, and Serna use trowels to work this grid.

Barring any surprises, we will close on the site on the 17th. We will leave Damnya Village on the 19th, move to Bayi on the 22nd; to Lhasa on the 24th; ship equipment to Beijing on the 25th – 27th, move to Beijing on the 28th, prepare reports, outbrief the Embassy staff, prepare equipment for shipment on 29 September through 1 October; depart Beijing for Hawaii on 2 October.   ≈ The team is baffled by finding pieces of clothing and other items but no remains. I called a former C-46 Hump pilot, Dr. Carl Constein. He explained that since the C-46 had an effective cockpit heating system, the crews at his base, Chabua, did not wear heavy flight suits and usually removed their flight jackets and pistol belts for comfort. He later e-mailed me after contacting George Wenrich, also a C-46 Hump pilot, who told him most pilots at Sookerating, where he was based, took with them in a duffle bag a winter fleece-lined flight uniform to be put on if they considered bailing out. This may explain why we are finding pieces of material and supports the team's theory that the crew bailed out.   ≈ The work here will be completed to standard.

CFC: When the phone rang at 9 p.m. (9 a.m. the next morning in Tibet) the day after I returned from Denver, I was excited to hear Geoff's voice. He was calling from the crash site.

Photo by Mike Swam

Geoff Kent calling the author from the crash site base camp to inquire about flight clothing crewmen wore. What the old Hump pilot told the captain in the satellite call and in a later e-mail was crucial information for Cap. Kent and the Anthropologist.

Photo by Mike Harris

Turning the tables on the official photographer, Mike Harris snaps his picture.

Photo by Mike Harris

(L to R) Geoff Kent, Mike Swam, and Al Castro work a grid, putting loose soil and surface stones into trashcans and buckets. The interested observer is Gumbo, the Tibetan hunter who discovered the crashed plane in 1999. What a connection that is.

Day 22
15 September
Crash Site

We completed four grid units. Significant items recovered include fabric, magazine from a 45 pistol, a zipper, and pieces of leather.

Day 23
16 September
Crash Site

After completing the last six grid units and drilling 25 test pits on the southern slope down from the crash, we closed the site. No remains were recovered during this operation.

Day 24
17 September
Final Base Camp

No scheduled activities.

Working the Grids

Photo by Dr. Tyrell

Seven Damnya laborers reflect their good spirits. In front of them are U.S. team members Behn and Harris. The Tibetans do not participate in actual site excavation.

Photo by Mike Harris

Bearded, on the way home now, Chris Behn sends birthday greetings to his wife.

25 Day
18 September
Final Base Camp

We began the breakdown of the camp, packed equipment and shipped non-essential equipment forward to Damnya Village with 30 porters. The Recovery Leader and the Photographer took photographs of material evidence. With the exception of the custom-made gun belt, all items were life-support material.   ≈ Rain his returned in time for our walk out beginning tomorrow.   ≈ We will send no further Sitreps until we reach Damnya Village on 21 September. We can continue to communicate via Iridium Pager and phone.

Day 26
19 September
Camp 2

We completed a five-hour movement to Camp 2, bypassing Camps 4 and 5 and crossing the river. In spite of heavy rainfall, the river was only knee-deep.

Day 27
20 September
Damnya Village

We completed a nine-hour movement. We decided to bypass Camp 1 and pushed on to Damnya Village, the thought of beer our incentive. After nine hours we arrived at Damnya at approximately 1730 hours.   ≈ The team is out of the mountains.

It's all downhill from here.

Getting ready for final movement.

Day 28
21 September
Damnya Village

We conducted phase 1 of Equipment Recovery, packing equipment and uploading equipment trucks. ≈ Additional comments: I saw a website link from SSG Gladhill of the Public Affairs Office concerning a Radio Australia news release: "China has recovered the wreckage of a World War II-era cargo plane that crashed in Tibet about 60 years ago." We believe this is our site, not a new one. Our concern is that the Chinese government released this information without our knowledge. The information is not completely accurate, particularly the comment about a lock of hair, which the Recovery Leader later determined to be hemp from a rope. Nor is there a mention in the release of the U.S.-China joint mission. ≈ The Chinese Team alternated two or three individuals daily at the site and sent 10 laborers daily to the site.

Day 29
22 September
Bayi Town

We arrived at Bayi Town at 1200 hours. We attended a banquet hosted by the prefectural government.

Day 30
23 September
Bayi Town

We completed final equipment recovery and packed it for shipment to Lhasa. ≈ Additional comments: Both the Team Recovery Leader and I addressed the media release of inaccurate information with the officials, explaining the sensitivity of such information and agreeing that such information should be corrected. We question whether the Chinese government received appropriate media guidance regarding MIA recovery operations and JPAC policies related to the release of scientific findings.

Back to the village for the first beer.

Swam, Gilbertson, Keohuhu-Bolor, Beemster, and Tyrell having their first beer.

Day 31
24 September
Lhasa

The team departed Bayi Town at 0800 hours and arrived in Lhasa at 1730 hours. We were greeted by Lhasa officials and Defense Attache Office representative. Over the next four days we will coordinate shipments of equipment to Beijing, be guests of Tibetan Autonomous Region officials, and conclude financial arrangements with the Chinese government. The team will fly to Beijing on 28 September. ≈ We received word that Philadelphia radio station KYW aired the report of a "Chinese Recovery."

∧∧∧

Larsen, Serna, and Morales slaking their thirst.

Mike Harris and Chris Behn enjoying their refreshments.

On the peak of Damnya Mountain are the Chinese team, locals, and the U.S. team.

Chinese and U.S. team leaders. (L to R) Mr. Targa, Capt. Kent, SFC Swam, Mr. Ma Zhijian.

Chapter 17

After-Action Reports

JOINT POW/MIA ACCOUNTING COMMAND
310 Worchester Avenue
Hickam AFB, Hawaii 96853-5530

14 December 2004

MEMORANDUM FOR: Commander, JPAC

SUBJECT: After-Action Package for Tibet 2004 Recovery Operation

1. The purpose of this package is not only to provide the command and staff with lessons learned on our Tibet Recovery Operation in 2004 but also to consolidate information concerning planning and logistics that can serve to provide continuity to planners and team leaders for future operations in China.

2. Included in this package are a number of support after-action reports written by persons who worked very hard to make this mission happen.

3. In the future, should another team leader be headed to this same region and he or she has any questions, I simply can be contacted

by email at james.kent@us.army.mil. I am ready to continue to serve this mission even when I have moved on in my career.

4. I consider myself very lucky to have had this opportunity to do this particular mission, certainly the highlight of my JPAC service.

James G. Kent, CPT,USA
Team Leader

Subject: Manning and Planning

Team Manning

Mission CH-03 was probably the highest-risk mission JPAC has conducted. C-46 #996 had crashed in a remote and inaccessible mountainous area of southeast Tibet. It was essential that the team be physically and mentally able to work effectively at high altitude. Extraction from the mountain of an injured person would be precarious, particularly because China does not allow foreign helicopters in its air space. A primary aim in manning was to select a highly qualified medical team that could bring the hospital to the field. Team members had complete confidence in Maj Karl Larsen, team physician and surgeon, and in medics MSgt Rocky Keohuhu-Bolor and SSgt Gabriel Serna. Dr. Larsen not only diagnosed/treated 79 cases on the mission, he was also mentor to the medics.

Selecting all team members, in fact, was a satisfying task, supported by Maj Washington, then-Operational Teams Chief. All 13 team members proved themselves physically fit, mentally tough, and able to function as a team.

Two mountaineers, Mark Gilbertson and SSgt Gary Beemster, were our insurance policy. Tough as nails, experienced at altitude, they served us well, on three occasions making installations to guide us through precarious passes and over wide, fast-flowing rivers.

Recommendations: 1. Insist on maximum physical and mental preparedness of all team members, including augmentees. Had we not washed out a linguist who did not measure up in mountain

166

training in Alaska, he might have prevented us from making it to the crash site. 2. Put on the team a physician who is also a surgeon.

CFC: Capt Kent sent me after-action reports of two other team members. With his concurrence, I have paraphrased and condensed all three military reports for civilian reading.

Coordination with U.S. Embassy

The U.S. Embassy in Beijing, China, one of the busiest in the world, is very supportive of JPAC. The Defense Attache was particularly helpful. However, the Embassy's emphasis is on matters of state. It cannot be bogged down in operational and logistical details of our missions. We are not the only show in town. A good Liaison Officer of our own, like GySgt Denny and MSgt MacMillan, can do our work.

Recommendation: Given the workload in China this year and the future, and considering work in North Korea, Beijing would be an excellent position for a Worldwide JPAC presence.

Team Leader/Planner

I was fortunate to be the principal planner as well as Team Leader for this mission. I had autonomy in planning and executing the operation, including selecting the team, and I had the complete support of PLOPS (Plans and Operations) Rick Hudson, Lt Col Buckingham, and Lt Col Orner. I am grateful for the opportunity, and I am proud of the mission.

Recommendation: I believe Team Leaders are underutilized. The Operational Plan should be ready two months prior to a worldwide mission so Team Leaders can be primary planners. If possible, Team Leaders should travel to host nations in advance for coordination and early face-to-face contact.

Subject: Team Training

Oahu Training Program

We underwent four weeks (May, 2004) of physical training, focusing on aerobic conditioning and leg strength. The weekly program included ruck marches/mountain hikes, running and weight-lifting, and "Triathlon Thursdays." Hikes built up to six hours with 60-pound packs.

Recommendation: Some movements in Tibet were 13 hours long with packs that weighed close to 100 pounds because of water saturation. To simulate the effect of altitude, training should be conducted at maximum heart rate for sustained periods.

Conditioning of Augmentees

To prepare for mountain training in Alaska, we brought in the augmentees to join our base staff team members in the Oahu training. Most augmentees were in good physical condition, but the two linguists were not. It was evident that one of them would not make it through mountain training.

Alaska Training

In November 2003 we requested a training program from the Northern Warfare Training Center. Our objects were to validate the team's preparedness for the mission, to validate and learn to use new equipment, and to learn basic mountaineering and cold-weather survival skills. NWTC provided a detailed rigorous program that helped us accomplish our goals. Although I agree with Recovery Leader Tyrell's comment in his report that the Alaska training did not exactly simulate conditions in Tibet (tough terrain coupled with altitude), for many of us the training movements in Alaska were the most demanding we had made in our military careers. NWTC planned and executed a first-rate program.

Recommendation: Maintain relationship with NWTC.

Subject: Mapping and Imagery/Weather

Mapping and Imagery

JPAC has a system in place for obtaining maps. However, we were not able to obtain satisfactory maps of Tibet through J2 (Planning). We networked outside the unit with Space Imaging, a commercial vendor, which provided excellent imagery and viewing software. In fact, when we arrived in Damnya Village, we felt we had already been there.

Recommendation: Satellite imagery contractors working at the Pacific Area Command are willing to assist JPAC. Team Leaders should be instructed on obtaining imagery outside JPAC if necessary.

Weather

The weather window for missions in southeast Tibet is smaller than we had anticipated. It wasn't until 10 September that the rain stopped. Travel by roads along the Yarlung River was precarious where the ground beneath had eroded into the river. Foot travel was dangerous because of wet rock. One person nearly had his thumb sliced off when he slipped at the crash site.

At the end of September the temperature dropped below freezing in the morning and we saw snow on 15,000-foot peaks.

Recommendation: The weather window for southeast Tibet missions should be 10-30 September. The Chinese will not work far into October because of the threat of snow.

Subject: Supply/Equipment, Compensation

Equipment Storage and Accountability

The equipment used by the Tibet 2002 team was poorly stored, most of it pilfered. Our team was required to purchase all new equipment. At the end of our mission we insisted the equipment be stored and secured in the J4 yard. (J 4 is Logistics/Budget.) Had we not done this, everything would have been issued out, along with "general issue."

Recommendations: 1. J4 should purchase ISU-type containers for storage. 2. Teams should maintain accountability of issued items, including mountaineering equipment.

Identifying Mountaineer/Camping Equipment

After receiving recommendations of the Northern Warfare Training Center in Fort Wainright, Alaska, we researched the items in Backpacker Magazine and online.

Recommendations: 1. Maintain contact with NWTC for recommendations. 2. Purchase second pair of boots for each team member.

Purchasing Equipment

Although it would have been simpler to purchase our equipment through POWER EDGE, located near the Ward Centre, we went the GSA contract route initiated at J4 and made a saving of $10k - $20k. We entered a contract with the small, high priority company MOUNTAIN GEAR in Spokane, Washington, at its low bid. Paul Fish, company CEO, cooperated in late purchases, including two bulk orders of dehydrated meals at discount prices. For local purchases, POWER EDGE is an excellent store for last-minute local purchases.

Recommendation: None

Validation of Equipment

NWTC mountaineers examined the equipment we had shipped to Alaska. On their recommendation, we purchased additional equipment in Alaska as required.

Recommendation: Take equipment to be used on recovery mission with you on mountain training mission for professional evaluation.

Negotiating Chinese Team's Budget and Expenses

I was afforded the opportunity as team leader/planner to travel to Beijing with Lt Col Buckingham, Mrs. Jennifer Nasarenko, and Mr. Aaron Lehl to negotiate operational and logistical requirements for three missions to China in Fiscal 04. Lt Col Buckingham handled the first two and then was tasked to Iraq. In his absence I led our delegation in negotiating with the Tibetans in Lhasa. It worked out well, for I considered it important for the Tibetan officials to see who carried the checkbook. When I returned in the summer, the Chinese team attempted to change several agreed-upon figures. I showed them the notes I had made in the negotiations in February; they dropped their case. Leading a delegation was an opportunity of a lifetime.

Recommendation: JPAC team leaders should travel in the group that discusses and later negotiates with the host country.

CFC: Included in Capt. Kent's After-Action Package is a 16-page Record of Employment of Local Laborers and Horses at Danniang *(Dymna) submitted by the Chinese. The record lists names (in Chinese and English) of laborers, dates and places of movements, purposes of assignments, labor costs for each movement, and total cost—408,000 Yen.*

The largest assignment was for 60 laborers to carry gear to Base Camp 3 and the Crash Site from August 28 through September 5. Other assignments included harnessing and driving 41 gear-carrying horses to Base Camp 1; carrying food, gear, buckets, and tents to both the American and Chinese teams; assisting in the investigation at the crash site.

Validation of Purchases by the Chinese Team

In negotiations we agreed on cost estimates for needed equipment. Recalling the bad record of storing and securing 2002 equipment, I stipulated that new items purchased were for the 2004 mission only and must be properly accounted for. We had made a 50 percent advance to the Chinese for purchases. When we arrived in

August to begin the mission, I discovered problems. Transportation rentals were unjustified, for we were using vehicles already owned. We were at first unable to locate the new vehicles. After I showed my counterpart that I was tracking daily vehicle accountability, I was taken to a roomful of the new equipment.

Recommendation: Make no greater advance payment than necessary for the Chinese to get up and moving.

> *CFC: In his memorandum package to the commander, Capt.Kent included a 3,000-word paper entitled* Chinese Negotiations. *The paper advises that U.S. negotiators carefully navigate the difference between Chinese and American culture in order to establish a business relationship. The four threads of thousands of years of Chinese culture are agrarianism, morality, pictographical language, and wariness of strangers. In spite of a lack of trust, the Chinese offer an opportunity for trust and friendship through casual conversation over a meal or cup of tea. During negotiations it is best to be patient, to avoid first-name informality, to avoid arrogance or lose composure, to expect slow-downs and 11th-hour changes. It is helpful to understand idiosyncrasies relating to numbers and colors. (Red brings good luck) U.S. negotiators need to pad the price in advance, to take copious notes, to realize that contracts in the Chinese mind are regarded as guidelines, not final legalities.*

Payments through the Embassy

Payments are made to the Chinese through the U.S. Embassy, Finance. JPAC is accustomed to making payments of this kind; the U.S. Embassy is not. This year's late payments caused a strain in U.S./JPAC and Chinese relations.

Recommendation: Before the start of any worldwide mission in which the Embassy will be involved with payments, it is essential that "our finance people talk to their finance people." Note: Chinese like payments to be made in U.S. dollars.

Subject: The Mission

Pre-Deployment (Passports and Visas)

We submitted application for passports and visas two months in advance. Visas will not be approved unless they have a "visa message" from the Chinese Ministry of Foreign Affairs in Beijing. Our visas were approved at the last minute, a common Chinese tactic.

Recommendations: 1. Collect passports from team members as early as practicable. 2. Submit passports for visa application soon after country clearance has been submitted. 3. Inform DAO representative and POL/MIL when and where you will submit your visa applications. 4. Continue to follow up with POL/MIL officer.

Deployment of Passengers and Equipment

The timing of aircraft lift for the DPRK (Democratic Peoples' Republic of Korea) missions enabled us to put our pallets of equipment on board a Milair aircraft. This went well. However, since Beijing is the only Chinese city currently open to U.S. Milair, a good deal of coordination by the J3 (Joint staff – Operations) planner with DAO for approval with the MFA is required. The same passport and visa scrutiny applies to the crew of the military transport. Commercial air transport is the better and easier way for passenger travel.

Recommendation: Micromanage the procedure re Milair.

Movement and Lack of Helicopter Support

Road movement was up to eight hours long, and our foot march from Damnya to the crash took us nearly five days. We packed light, hiring enough local labor to carry all team equipment to the site. Since China does not approve the use of foreign helicopters, a serious problem was lack of medevac support. We estimated it would take a week to carry an injured man out. Ultimately, we were lucky.

Recommendation: I take full responsibility for recommending our mission to the commander. Upon completion of the mission, I recommend no further operations to remote sites in which helicopter medevac is not available.

Relationships Among Leaders

Dr. Andy Tyrell, SFC Mike Swam, and I meshed extremely well. We demonstrated respect for one another and supported one another in our clearly defined responsibilities Dr. Tyrell was a pleasure to work with. He trained hard as a member of the team. The team appreciated his common sense approach and his clear strategy for recovery. SFC Swam is superb. A by-the-book, dress right-dress- type guy, he established that he was in charge from training through excavation. True to the Non-Commissioned Officers' Code, he enabled both Dr. Tyrell and me to focus on our duties.

Recommendation: It is essential that team leaders get together prior to beginning a mission to establish boundaries. The Team Sergeant runs the team, the Recovery Leader is in charge of the site, the buck stops with the Team Leader.

Subject: Communication Equipment

Satcom Package

From After-Action Reports of previous missions, we learned of communications equipment failures. We therefore put together a redundant package which included two Inmarsats, three iridium phones, two iridium pagers, one worldwide cell phone, and one laptop computer configured for data transport via Satcom.

Inmarsat worked well. Working with the Citrex server, we were able to communicate via email from one of the most remote regions on the globe. But Citrex was very slow. For our reports back to JPAC, we typed a Word document then cut and pasted it to email prior to sending. Inmarsat batteries, unfortunately, worked for only two or three calls then required a long charge.

The Iridiums phones were excellent and essential for morale for calls to the office and home. The downside was signal strength and intermittent cut-offs on almost every call.

The Iridium pager was a must, receiving phone pages and text messages from the internet and emails as well. To conserve battery strength on our phones, we left the pagers on. If someone needed to call, they would send a page. Every morning before going to the crash site, we shared news and sports received in text form.

The Worldwide cell phone worked well and had coverage in Beijing and Lhasa.

The Panasonic Ultra-Tough is a durable, waterproof computer. Its disadvantage is its difficult-to-use keyboard.

Recommendations: (1) Look for an alternate laptop that is equally tough and waterproof but more user-friendly. (2) Look for stronger Inmarsat batteries, high-powered iridium antennas. (3) Work connectivity and speed issues with Inmarsat/Citrex and data transmission. (4) Team leaders should know and practice data transmission via satellite communications.

Public Affairs

Chinese News Release

The U.S. Embassy in Beijing asked for guidance on handling information regarding the joint U.S./Chinese recovery mission. We received no guidance to be passed on to the Embassy. Without our knowledge, China released incorrect and misleading information regarding the recovery mission. This release made it to Australian news agencies and was later heard on radio in Philadelphia.

Recommendation: (1) The Public Affairs Office should prepare media guidance for foreign country hosts. It should be polished by J5 (Joint staff – Policy) and introduced during strategic and Operation/Logistics discussions.

Dr. Carl Frey Constein

DEPARTMENT OF THE AIR FORCE
10th Medical Group
USAF Academy, Colorado

5 October 2004

NEMORANDUM FOR: CPT Geoff Kent
JPAC/SG
10MDOS/CC

FROM: MAJ Karl Larsen
Team Tibet Surgeon

All medical team members participated in medical support and coordinated with each other on a daily basis to ensure appropriate continuity. The main types of medical support and capabilities included on-demand sick-call, emergency medical and surgical treatment, public health monitoring and inspection (including food-preparation areas in Damnya village), monitoring of responses to high-altitude exposure, prophylaxis and treatment of altitude-induced illness, and high-angle rescue, treatment and extrication.

Based on augmentee surgeon's (Col Bart Iddins) recommendations from the previous high-altitude mission to Tibet, a specially tailored medical package was constructed to provide comprehensive medical support and still be transportable. Unique to this mission, special emphasis was placed on bringing a portable altitude chamber (PAC), recovery equipment (SKEDCO and KED) specifically designated altitude illness treatment and prophylaxis medications, and emergency trauma equipment. In consideration of the remote nature and prolonged extraction that would be required in the event of severe injury during the team's time on the mountains, an external fixation set was brought to stabilize major skeletal trauma during an estimated seven-day extraction time. The entire package was transportable by four or five laborers.

Seventy-nine medical conditions were diagnosed/treated. Among them were
> Upper respiratory infection/sinusitis
> Partial rotator cuff tear

> Anterior knee pain
> Mild , moderate, and severe Acute Mountain
>   Sickness (AMS)
> Acute gastroenteritis (AGE)
> Failure to adapt to altitude
> Chest wall contusion
> Hand and thumb laceration
> Paronychiae of thumb and middle finger
> Finger infection
> Severe headache
> Second-degree burn
> Forearm contusion/suspect fracture
> Gastrointestinal fracture
> General conditions affecting all U.S. Team members
>   -- weight loss of 3 to 15 pounds
>   ---nocturnal periodic respiration

Malaria

The team was given a last-minute issue of doxycycline malaria prophylaxis prior to the main body deploying to Beijing. This was not coordinated with the team surgeon and was unnecessary. Major cities in China do not present a malaria risk, and mosquito vectors are found at altitudes below 1500 meters.

Recommendation: Future high-altitude deployments should take into account the actual team exposure risk to malaria. If a risk exists, a preventive regimen should be coordinated with the team physician/ medics and should be implemented well ahead of deployment.

Acute Gastroenteritis (AGE)

The attack rate of AGE was nearly 50 percent (6/13 personnel). Many of these cases were probably acquired from airline food or food served at dinners. Several were suspected to be related to food from street-side stands. In a unit that frequently deploys to third-world environments, one would expect more caution.

Recommendation: Avoid street stands; consume only hot foods from inspected facilities and clean-appearing restaurants.

Emergency Equipment Ahead of U.S. Team

Laborers were capable of traveling much faster than the rest of the team. As a result, those laborers carrying emergency medical equipment were ahead and out of reach of the U.S. team.

Recommendations: (1) Constantly monitor those laborers carrying important equipment on the marches. (2) Provide the labor team leader with a radio.

Medical Gear Wet

In spite of being packed in plastic boxes in "waterproof" duffle bags, all medical gear became significantly wet during the trip. Much of it will be unusable on return to Hickam. The primary cause of the problem was heavy, unrelenting rain, at times overcoming waterproof zippers. In addition, some laborers put their own equipment into the duffle bags, the bags had to opened to retrieve supplies, and until the space-station tent arrived at the excavation campsite, there was little shelter to protect the bags.

Recommendations: Options: (1) Use wet-weather bags/rucksacks as used by USAF pararescue. (2) Double-bag. (3) Use small pelican cases. (4) Use large shelters, tarpaulins.

Oxygen Unavailable at Excavation Site

It was not discovered until the pallets were broken down in Damnya that two portable oxygen cylinders, part of the initial package, became separated from the medical gear. Fortunately, oxygen was not required on the mission.

Recommendation: The portable oxygen systems programmed to travel with Team Tibet should be used in the future, with more attentive tracking of the cylinders.

Chinese Physician Out of Action

The lead Chinese physician returned to Damnya because of altitude-related issues. Many Chinese team medicine labels became lost in the rain, rendering some of the powdered medicines useless. We were frequently called to care for the Chinese team and laborers, requiring a one-hour descent to the Chinese camp, or a one-hour climb by the Chinese individual to the U.S. camp.

Recommendation: Future joint USA/foreign national medical coverage should continue to include robust medical support to care for all of the U.S./foreign national members involved. The Chinese need to consider how the event that occurred can be precluded.

Prophylaxis for Altitude Illness

Prophylaxis was used before travel to Lhasa, continued for three days then stopped, to be started again after crossing the first mountain pass. However, the altitude of the first crossing was actually 14,800 feet rather than 14,300 as stated in data provided from the initial investigation, the duration of the trip was 14 hours rather than five, and the time spent at altitude longer. Even so, the prophylaxis used reduced the mountain sickness to about 25 – 30 percent.

Recommendation: Use the appropriate medication and dosage starting the night before a climb, continue during travel, and for 3 – 5 days after arrival at the final altitude.

Acclimatization to Altitude Varies

Certain team members demonstrated repetitive episodes of altitude illness. It raises concern about the individual's ability to function in future high-altitude missions without more intense medical attention.

Recommendation: Give consideration to the incidence of high-altitude illness or lack of it in team members when planning future high-altitude missions or establishing any sort of permanent mountain/high-altitude team.

DEPARTMENT OF THE ARMY
U.S. Army Alaska Northern Warfare Training Center
1060 Gaffney Road
Fort Wainright, AK 99703-9900
04 October 2004

MEMORANDUM FOR RECORD

SUBJECT: After-Action Review for JPAC #CH-03

The investigation of this crash site in 2002 proved there could be a water obstacle requiring the use of ropes to make a safe river crossing three days out of Damnya. Factors affecting river height include glacier melt-off, rain, and time of day. It was also determined that a small section of narrow ledges near a waterfall may have needed a hand line for safe crossing. The possibility of moving large pieces of aircraft wreckage at the crash site was also discussed.

River Crossing

The river was hazardous to cross on foot because of its depth and rapid pace. It was decided to wait until morning when the river would be at its lowest level. Early the next day a U.S. mountaineer and a Tibetan mountaineer crossed on foot and constructed a rope bridge farther up the river. The American and the Chinese/Tibetan teams crossed successfully.

Recommendation: Use a hand-thrown safety device for a crossing farther downstream.

Precarious Ledge

On day five out of Damnya the route crossed to the right of a waterfall. The path was precarious, as narrow as a few inches at some places. A fixed line was required for safety. After I drilled a hole into the wall at the start of the proposed line, the Tibetan mountaineer hitched several clusters of alders for intermediate anchors. Several pitons were used for another intermediate anchor and the final anchor. The Tibetan mountaineer was confused about the suitability of several of his anchors. After a lengthy period of rerouting ropes and retying anchors, the problems were eventually resolved.

Recommendation: Hand drills prove too slow in these situations in southeast Tibet. A powered masonry drill is recommended.

Moving Aircraft Wreckage

To move parts of the aircraft wreckage for thorough excavation, anchors were inserted on the cliff near the crash site, using two three-point equalized anchors with two hangers and one piton per anchor. One-inch webbing equalized the anchors and extended them beyond the rock face. The anchors were attached to two separate ropes and two separate come-alongs. After anchors were attached to the wreckage, slack was taken out of the rope system using transport-tightening systems on each rope. The come-alongs were insufficient to move the wreckage. One of the bolts failed under stress. When it was realized that the wreckage could not be moved sideways, a large number of U.S. and Tibetan team members pushed the wreckage downhill.

Recommendations: (1) To move large pieces of aircraft wreckage requires a winch of suitable power and a generator to run it. (2) A second option is a gas-operated metal-cutting tool to chop the wreckage into pieces. Such equipment was not available on this mission.

POC for this memorandum is SSG Gary Beemster at (907) 353-1165.

Chapter 18

Excerpts from

Geoff's Journal

<u>MOVEMENT TO BAYI.</u> On our drive from Lhasa to Bayi our convoy consisted of three buses, a luggage van, two equipment trucks, and two land cruisers. I rode in the lead cruiser with Targa, leader of the Chinese team. It was an eight-hour wild ride, loud speaker screaming as we sped through village after village.

≈ *We saw historical places, including Gamaging Village, birthplace of King Songsten Gampo, the king who unified Tibet in the 7th century.*

As we headed east, the scenery became spectacular, the landscape greener, the trees taller, the water bluer. Bayi is a little Chinese city. The dress of the locals was more contemporary, the homes more modern...clearly the influence of the Chinese had taken hold in eastern Tibet. Largely populated by Szechuan immigrants, the town sported shops, restaurants, even karaoke bars!

Met with officials...official speeches by both parties...

The Chinese mostly concentrated on "bi-lateral cooperation between our two countries."

<u>DAMNYA VILLAGE.</u> Looked like it came straight out of the old west...much interest in us Americans by the villagers, especially the children...a lot of curiosity...a couple stores, a kitchen, a bar. ≈

Rented enough beds for the team at $1.00 a night. Slept on make-shift boxes and foam pads in rooms like wooden boxes large enough for two, much like prison cells...amused by idea of a sheep sleeping at the end of the hall. Locals in this village very poor...so poor women made purses out of old basketballs.

FIRST DAY OF MOVEMENT. Walked 16 kilometers (nearly 10 miles), six hours, crossing a steam several times. Walked into the rain.

SECOND DAY OF MOVEMENT. This was our toughest day. Based on a 2002 site and route investigation, we expected this movement to be four to six hours long . We were wrong. It turned out to be a long, long day and a treacherous journey. ≈ *We started at Camp 1 and climbed straight up for hours. As we climbed with our 60-pound packs, we wondered whether it was aerobic activity or just oxygen deprivation that had us breathing so hard. It was both. You absolutely had to be in great shape to handle this trek—no trail, straight up, sometimes on all fours, in the initial climb through the forest.*

We approached a cliff and overhang that thankfully took us out of the rain. Local laborers made a fire. Our guide was a Tibetan mountaineer who had scaled Everest several times. He didn't speak much but he had mastered the phrase, "Slowly, Slowly."... we in our top-of-the-line hiking boots, he in his running sneakers, villagers in cheap canvas shoes with flat soles having little tread. These porters--small men and boys, no rain gear—bolted through the trail with the rest of our equipment slung on their backs with nothing but canvas straps and ropes...these were the toughest men I've ever seen.

As we approached 13.5 k, it was extremely difficult to breathe and climb. We took breaks every half-hour, but only for 10 minutes to catch our breath.. Finally, around 4 in the afternoon, we reached the summit of Damnya Mountain. ≈ We had split into two groups, communicating by radio, unaware of the distance between us. Once our group got over the crest we realized we had only four or five hours of daylight left. It was raining and cold, about 40 degrees, visibility about 50 feet. We were lost in the clouds. Even the guides had difficulty figuring out where we were. Somehow we had gone off course, costing us precious time.

As we moved down from the summit it became clear that the second group had not yet reached the summit and was having problems with altitude. We learned later that Harris was vomiting and Rocky had become delirious. We thought he hadn't had enough sugar so Gunny gave Rocky a candy bar. I was with the lead group. We decided to stay put and wait until the second group caught up, and we'd move the rest of the way together. ≈ We waited a long two hours. When they arrived, we had only an hour or two of daylight left. With two of our men suffering AMS, we had no choice but to push down the mountain—*in the dark!*

Rocky was still suffering. SFC Swam called for Doc Larsen to come take a look at him. Meanwhile, we were climbing around 100-foot dead drops. Despite being exhausted, every one of us had to be sharp and alert. We turned on our head lamps and proceeded. The rocks were wet...our walking extremely dangerous. Mountaineers Beemster and Gilbertson were worth their weight in gold—absolutely essential to our survival. They recognized especially precarious spots along the way and guided each of us—literally foot by foot—on the rocks. ≈ I slipped on a rock, fell headfirst, and bounced off several rocks. I lay in an awkward position. Gabe Serna asked me if I was all right. "I think so," I said, "but I need help to get up." I was spared serious injury only because of the large pack I had on my back. Finally at about 2200 hours we arrived at the spot by the river for Camp 2. After 13 hours of the toughest hiking any one us had ever done, we barely had enough energy to put up the tents. We were lucky to get through this terrible day without injury.

THIRD AND FOURTH DAYS OF MOVEMENT
Another long and grueling day. We had a 14,600-foot peak to cross and a dangerous pass along a cliff face to negotiate. The weather continued foggy and wet. ≈ A major problem was developing...Mike Harris began walking more slowly and showing symptoms of Acute Mountain Sickness. His condition worsened as we continued to climb. Doc Larsen advised that we get him over the 13,500-foot peak and down as quickly as possible. Unfortunately, the medical gear had gone

forward with the porters. ≈ *Our packs weighed nearly 100 pounds now because they were saturated by rain . Mike dropped his pack and we had a porter carry it. At the next break I noticed Mike's nose was running and he was breathing extremely hard. He continued to march on his own without a pack until we got to about 200 feet beneath the pass. Two men assisted him as we crossed the peak and began our descent. At about 13,000 feet he started moving on his own. For the next several hours we descended on Camp 4.* ≈ I note this as the most courageous display during the mission. Harris was all guts. He was hurting more than anyone could imagine. Fighting AMS and physical exhaustion of climbing this terrain at nearly 15,000 feet, he never gave up. He knew how dangerous this movement was for him. He put all his trust and confidence, even his life, in the hands of the team leadership. When we arrived at Camp 4, just 1500 below the crash site, we knew the worst of the journey was over. ≈ *We made a decision to take a team rest day the next day. With medication and rest, Harris was able to arrive at the crash site two days later. His AMS did not recur.*

From the camp site we could look up at what appeared to be one of the plane's engines far down the slope close to the camp, probably there by gravitational pull. Our reaction was, "This is it... we're here." We could hardly wait to get into the cockpit of that plane.

The next morning we conducted a leaders' survey, climbing about two hours to reach the crash. Mike Swam and I scouted out a final base camp just below the crash site while Andy Tyrell, with the assistance of Behn, Castro, and Serna, surveyed the site. Five porters went with us—Bobo, Denzi, Mema, Gumbo, and Puba. Bobo became very special to us and became a good friend of Swam. The porters move much faster than we did. Bobo was always the one waiting for us, helping us with our weight and leading us to the site. ≈ As wet and cold as the rest of us, the porters were nonplused by the elements and the conditions. Hard and difficult—this is their life. They know nothing different. Gumbo, whom I befriended, was in fact the Tibetan hunter who discovered the crash years ago. He pointed out the area where he had found the pistol. I was so excited I wanted to walk right over there and take a look. But this was Andy

Tyrell's baby, and I respected the process of how he wanted to go about it. Andy established the site like a crime scene where we would methodically search 3m x 3m grids, working left to right and upwards. It was exciting to be at the crash site, even more exciting to establish our final base camp and organize to do the job we came for.

"Aluminum Trail" is an apt term for the trail left by the many planes that crashed on the Hump. Here at the site we saw aluminum torn into twisted fragments, some large, many small, some recognizable, most not. At first glance we could make out a wing section or part of the fuselage, two intact propellers, probably an indication that they were not moving at impact. This supported the theory that the plane ran out of gas. Much of the wreckage was concentrated in one area, although engines and heavy parts had moved farther down the mountain, almost 1,000 feet below. The plane appeared to have been flying in a northerly direction when it crashed. Andy found the vertical stabilizer with the plane's number visible, confirming it was indeed the plane we were searching for. What struck me was that the men who flew the Hump flew in an aircraft with so thin a covering.

THE BEST DAY. Except when we crawled into our sleeping bags at the end of the day, we were completely soaked by 10 continuous days of rain. On some nights we dried our boots by a campfire near the Chinese camp. It became a ritual to put up our tents, take off our socks and wring them out, then hang them up for the night. We kept one dry pair in our sleeping bags for sleeping.

One morning Mike Swam and I woke up to a lot of noise and confusion. Rocky was singing something that sounded like, "I can see clearly now the rain is gone." We all gave him the Bronx Cheer... until we spied a ray of sunlight in the tent. We jumped out and saw the most magnificent mountain view, the Himalayan peaks of India off in the distance, highlighted against a glorious blue sky. We were so happy we delayed going to work until noon, meanwhile pulling out all our belongings from the tents, emptying our rucks, hanging everything out to dry, charging phone batteries with the solar charger, taking pictures, enjoying life. For me, it was the happiest moment in recent memory.

WORST DAY. Our happiest day was soon displaced by our worst. There was nothing special about it, but one day we just kind of knew it wasn't looking good for finding human remains. The mood was solemn, no one even talking as we worked. We returned to the base camp late that afternoon, cooked our dinner meals and went to bed. It took a couple days to get over our depression. *≈ Then we began speculating about what happened to the crew of the C-46. My call to Dr. Constein pretty well confirmed that the fragments of material we were finding came from heavier flight suits pilots stuffed into duffle bags for emergencies. The crew had bailed out. So be it. We could feel pride in the tough training and hard work we endured on the recovery mission of a lifetime, one of the most precarious high-risk operations ever for JPAC. Still...none of us will forget that sad September day. We would rather have made more 13-hour movements of grave danger than feel the disappointment of that day.*

CAMP LIFE. When we arrived at the final base camp, we had already gone a week without shaving or cleaning ourselves, there being no place in the village to shower or even go to the bathroom. We continued to wear the same wet clothes. Our command decision was not to shave on this mission in order to keep natural oil on the skin and to avoid infection from shaving cuts. *≈ At the final base camp we had a running water source we used for drinking, cooking, and brushing teeth. We set up a community toilet in the distance for use with bio-degradable garbage bags. We did not urinate in these bags. When they were filled, the bags were taken to the trash point and burned.*

Our Mountain Hardware tents were set up for the two-man buddy team's convenience. They were large, with plenty room for a vestibule where we could leave our boots and at times do our cooking. Some of the guys laid flat rock in the vestibule. Others dug into the shallow soil to level it for sleeping. The buddy-group plan worked well, tent groups often boiling enough water for themselves and others or for a community meal setting. *≈ Every morning after wake-up, we ate, packed a lunch meal, and met for a pre-work meeting run by Team Sergeant Mike Swam. We went over the day's events and* *shared news from home I found on email, internet, or satellite pager. From Hawaii I received text messages on news and sports scores. We tracked the opening weeks of NCAA basketball and NFL football... huge for morale.*

We discussed pertinent issues—medical, mountaineering, recovery, and others. Each member had a lane of experience that gave him decision-making authority—regardless of rank. I found this worked well in that we never stifled another's initiative. ≈ *We worked the site until 1500 or 1600 hours, depending on the day's progress. When we worked, we really moved. Everyone took his turn getting into "the hole" working hard, moving rock and soil. When a man got tired, someone was there to rotate in. This work ethic freed Andy to collect his scientific data. When we completed a grid, Andy checked it and gave us the nod to take photographs and move on to the next.* ≈ When we returned to camp at the end of the day, we boiled water and ate our dehydrated meals. We got turned on to Mountain House Meals in Alaska and bulk-ordered them for the mission. After dinner a couple guys would hang out and "talk story," as Rocky put it in his Hawaiian vernacular. Others would go to their tents to read, write, play cards or call home, although most made their morale calls in the morning because of the time difference. Of course if it rained we stayed in our tents. Connected to a satellite antenna outside, I worked in my tent to make Sitrep reports to the command and the U.S. Embassy in Beijing.

THE NON-COM IN CHARGE

Sergeant First Class Mike Swam ran the daily meetings, and I do mean ran! He insisted on everyone being on time. That included me, I felt. Here I am, I thought, close to a panic mode worrying about getting to my sergeant's meeting on time...tells you the respect I have for the guy. ≈ *The fact is, I led the team but he ran it. This is the way the Non-Commissioned Officers' Code intended it. He did everything right—keeping things organized, running work schedules, keeping the guys on track, keeping up group morale, working with the Chinese.*

Mike is perhaps the finest non-commissioned officer I have served with. Beyond that, he's like an older brother to me, and I love him like one. As tent mates, we got to know each other well, talking, sharing stories night after night. I teased about how meticulous he was. My side of the tent was chaos—a book here, a dirty spoon there, a dirty sock hanging here or there. His area was always neat, things lined up for the next day...probably comes from his Ranger days. I envied what I called his compulsion.

On that dark day when, hope against hope, we admitted we would find no remains, Mike had the right stuff to help the team over the disappointment. We held our heads high as we left the mountain for the last time.

Epilogue

Morale was high as the men of Team Tibet 2004 deployed to the Himalayas. At the crash site on the roof of the world, they set about their arduous task of searching for remains. Their work was spiritual as well as physical; they shared with families of the aircrew a deep desire for closure. Sadly, on this mission it was not to be.

As a Hump pilot, I feel the sorrow of the team and the families. But I am heartened by the enduring American spirit that motivates these searches. I salute the valiant, caring men of Team Tibet 2004 and their JPAC Command. An MIA mission is a profound metaphor for the sacredness of each life.

I now more fully appreciate this meditation of John Donne:

> *Any man's death diminishes me;*
> *I am involved in Mankind.*
> *Therefore never send to know*
> *For whom the bell tolls.*
> *It tolls for thee.*

Also by Carl Frey Constein

Born to Fly the Hump
The author, a WWII pilot, recalls his 96
missions over the mighty Himalayas.
(Memoir)

Orchestra Left, Row T
An injured WWII Hump pilot calls on his love
of wine, women, and song to survive civilian life.
(Novel)_

Sadie's Place
In the decade of the Sizzling Sixties, a superintendent of schools
struggles to balance the will of students, staff, board, and
community.
(Novel)

Tales of the Himalayas
WWII airmen who flew the Hump and other veterans
of the China-Burma-India theater tell their stories.
(Letters)

War Memories and Civilian Musings
The author sees connections
between his war experiences and civilian life.
(Reflections)

Acknowledgments

I am indebted to JPAC (Joint Prisoner of War/ Missing in Action Accounting Command) and to several CBI fellow-veterans for their important help in writing this book. I extend my special appreciation to:

Capt Geoffrey Kent and members of Team Tibet 2004 for undertaking this mission. I owe my deepest gratitude to Geoff for inviting me to dialogue with him, for keeping me advised by e-mail and telephone along the way, and for sending me copies of sitreps and other reports—and nearly 100 magnificent photographs! I particularly appreciate his gracious response to my requests for information. He and his team delivered on the promise to represent Hump crews "with the same sense of duty, honor, respect, and courage we demonstrated 60 years ago."

Marvin K. Bortz, friend, fellow CBI C-46 pilot stationed in China. (Read his letter on pages 97-99 of my *Tales of the Himalayas*.) I thank him for processing 80-some graphics and captions, for being a meticulous copyreader, and for rescuing me from the arcane nether world of the computer. Given to efforts at wit and repartee, we kept our work sessions light, often joshing about that all-important condition of the military—rank. A captain, Marvin outranked me, a 1st lieutenant, one step from the bottom.

Geroge A. Wenrich, Ashburn, Virginia, Lt Col (Retired), college friend, for photographs of Sookerating and the Hump, and especially for providing information about extra clothing that Sookerating pilots took with them on their flights. Team Leader Geoff Kent and Anthropologist Andy Tyrell greatly appreciated this vital information, which I sent them by e-mail directly to the site. It explained why the team was finding so many pieces of clothing but no remains and confirmed their theory that the crew had bailed out.

J. V. Vinyard, Amarillo, Texas, president of the China-Burma-India Hump Pilot Association, who answered my questions about CBI

Hump and Air Force history, supplied information about Sookerating, sent me good photographs, gave me useful hints, and led me to people who were of further help.

Wendall A. Phillips, Whitehall, Pennsylvania, National Chaplain of the CBI Veterans Association, for supplying books about the CBI, charts, Army Post Offices, radio call letters/frequencies, and other data on all bases in the CBI; and for answering my frequent questions about the work of flight radio operators in the CBI.

Bob Smith, Flatrock, North Carolina, radio operator who was based in Sookerating, for helping me better understand the relationship between the flight radio operator and ground control, both on routine flights as well as in emergencies.

Reading PA Public Library for obtaining out-of-print and out-of-circulation books for my research.

Bibliography

Bradley, James. *Flyboys.* Little, Brown and Company, 2003

Brokaw, Tom. *The Greatest Generation.* Random House, 1998

Christy, Joe and Page Shamburger. *Summon the Stars.* A. S. Barnes and Company, 1970

Constein, Carl Frey. *Born to Fly the Hump.* 1st Books Library, 2001

_____. *Tales of the Himalayas.* 1st Books Library, 2002

Downie, Don and Jeff Ethell. *Flying the Hump.* Motorbooks International, 1996

Dmitri, Ivan. *Flight to Everywhere.* Whittlesey House, 1944

Gress, Robert J. *Milkrun.* Cross-Cultural Communications, 1995

Hengshoon, Harry. *Green Hell.* B & L Lithograph, 2000

Joint POW/MIA Accounting Command. *Until They Are Home.* http://www.jpac.pacom.mil/

Koenig, William. *Over the Hump.* Ballantine Books, 1972

Moser, Don. *China-Burma-India.* Time-Life Books, 1978

Pyle, Richard and Horst Faas. *Lost over Laos.* Da Capo Press, 2003

Quinn, Chick Marrs. *The Aluminum Trail.* Self-published, 1989

Schultz, Duane P. *The Doolittle Raid.* St. Martin's Press, 1988

Severeid, Eric. *Not so Wild a Dream.* Knopf, 1946

Spencer, Otha C. *Flying the Hump.* Texas A & M Press, 1995

_____. *Flying the Weather.* The Country Studio, 1996

Starks, Richard and Miriam Murcutt *Lost in Tibet.* Lyons Press, 2004

Swift, Earl. *Where They Lay.* Houghton Mifflin, 2003

Thorne, Bliss K. *The Hump.* Lippincott, 1965

Tunner, William B. *Over the Hump.* Duell, Sloan, Pearce, 1964

White, Edwin Lee. *Ten Thousand Tons by Christmas.* Walkytie, 1975.

White, Theodore and Annalee Jacoby. *Thunder out of China.* Sloan, 1946

About the Author

Carl Frey Constein was born in the eastern Pennsylvania town of Fleetwood in 1920. After graduating from college, he enlisted in the Army Air Corps as an Aviation Cadet. He received his pilot's wings and 2nd Lieutenant's Commission at Waco, Texas, in 1944 and was sent to India to fly supplies and materiel to China across the Himalayan Hump. For his 96 C-46 missions, he was awarded two Air Medals and the Distinguished Flying Cross.

After the war Constein earned a doctorate at Temple University in English and Educational Administration. He has been an English teacher, director of curriculum, superintendent of schools, and education writer. He is the author of six books.

Dr. Constein lives in Wernersville, near Reading, PA. He lectures frequently about the WWII Hump and the China-Burma-India theater of operations.

Printed in the United States
36744LVS00003B/289-291

9 781420 836943